GROWING DEEP IN THE CHRISTIAN LIFE
RETURNING TO OUR ROOTS

BIBLE STUDY GUIDE

From the Bible-teaching ministry of

Charles R. Swindoll

INSIGHT FOR LIVING

Charles R. Swindoll is a graduate of Dallas Theological Seminary and has served in pastorates for more than twenty-three years, including churches in Texas, New England, and California. Since 1971 he has served as senior pastor of the First Evangelical Free Church of Fullerton, California. Chuck's radio program, "Insight for Living," began in 1979. In addition to his church and radio ministries, Chuck has written twenty-one books and numerous booklets on a variety of subjects.

Based on the outlines of Chuck's sermons, the study guide text is coauthored by Bill Watkins, a graduate of California State University at Fresno and Dallas Theological Seminary. The Living Insights are written by Bill Butterworth, a graduate of Florida Bible College, Dallas Theological Seminary, and Florida Atlantic University. Bill Butterworth is currently the director of counseling ministries at Insight for Living.

Editor in Chief:	Cynthia Swindoll
Coauthor of Text:	Bill Watkins
Author of Living Insights:	Bill Butterworth
Editorial Assistant:	Karene Wells
Copy Manager:	Jac La Tour
Senior Copy Assistant:	Jane Gillis
Copy Assistant:	Glenda Schlahta
Director, Communications Division:	Carla Beck
Project Manager:	Nina Paris
Art Director:	Becky Englund
Production Artists:	Karen Hall and Donna Mayo
Typographer:	Bob Haskins
Cover Designer:	Walvoord, Killion, Edmonson & Hanlon, Inc.
Photographers:	Dave Edmonson, Photri, and Steve Terrill
Print Production Manager:	Deedee Snyder
Printer:	Frye and Smith

Unless otherwise identified, all Scripture references are from the New American Standard Bible, © The Lockman Foundation 1960, 1962, 1963, 1968, 1971, 1972, 1973, 1975, 1977. Used by permission.

ISBN 0-88070-189-7

Ordering Information

An album that contains twenty-two messages on eleven cassettes and corresponds to this study guide may be purchased through Insight for Living, Post Office Box 4444, Fullerton, California 92634. For ordering information, please refer to the order form at the end of this study guide. If the form has been removed, simply write to our office or call (714) 870-9161 to receive a current catalog and ordering information.

Canadian residents may obtain a catalog and ordering information through Insight for Living Ministries, Post Office Box 2510, Vancouver, British Columbia, Canada V6B 3W7, (604) 272-5811. Overseas residents should direct their correspondence to our Fullerton office.

If you wish to order by Visa or MasterCard, you are welcome to use our toll-free number, (800) 772-8888, Monday through Friday between the hours of 8:30 A.M. and 4:00 P.M., Pacific time. This number may be used anywhere in the continental United States except Alaska, California, and Hawaii. Orders from these areas can be made by calling our general office number, (714) 870-9161. Orders from Canada can be made by calling (604) 272-5811.

Table of Contents

Growing Deep in the Christian Life

The first Psalm describes a person who has strength of character, who delights in the Lord, who walks with God. The psalmist pictures such an individual as being

> *. . . like a tree firmly planted by streams of water,*
> *Which yields its fruit in its season,*
> *And its leaf does not wither. . . . (Ps. 1:3)*

What is it that gives a tree its stability? How can that tree continue to withstand incredible windstorms? Where is its major source of nourishment? In its roots . . . those deep, tough tentacles that grip the earth and seek out water.

Christians who stand firm, who resist the childish tendency to get swept off their feet by the winds of false teaching, are those who have strong doctrinal roots. They know what they believe. They are secure in their faith. They refuse to be uprooted.

The messages in this study take us back to the basics. They address most of the major doctrines of our evangelical faith. You will want to have your Bible handy as we cultivate the soil around these roots. I have done my best to keep each doctrine interesting. My desire is that you will do your best to apply each doctrine, personally.

Chuck Swindoll

Putting Truth into Action

Knowledge apart from application falls short of God's desire for His children. Knowledge must result in change and growth. Consequently, we have constructed this Bible study guide with these purposes in mind: (1) to stimulate discovery, (2) to increase understanding, and (3) to encourage application.

At the end of each lesson is a section called *Living Insights.* There you'll be given assistance in further Bible study, and you'll be encouraged to contemplate and apply the things you've learned. This is the place where the lesson is fitted with shoe leather for your walk through the varied experiences of life.

It's our hope that you'll discover numerous ways to use this tool. Some useful avenues we suggest are personal meditation, joint discovery, and discussion with your spouse, family, work associates, friends, or neighbors. The study guide is also practical for Sunday school classes, Bible study groups, and, of course, as a study aid for the "Insight for Living" radio broadcast.

In order to derive the greatest benefit from this process, we suggest that you record your responses to the lessons in the space which has been provided for you. In view of the kinds of questions asked, your study guide may become a journal filled with your many discoveries and commitments. We anticipate that you will find yourself returning to it periodically for review and encouragement.

Bill Watkins
Coauthor of Text

Bill Butterworth
Author of Living Insights

GROWING DEEP IN THE CHRISTIAN LIFE

RETURNING TO OUR ROOTS

The Value of Knowing the Scoop
Selected Scripture

Theology—to many people, just the word sparks visions of dusty, old, thick books filled with exacting jargon that does more for curing insomnia than for clarifying truth. *Boring, unrelentingly complex, irrelevant, impractical*—these are frequently the adjectives used to describe doctrine. But does the study of Christian theology have to be like this? Must it be dull and tedious—presented as if it has little to do with daily life? Not at all! Indeed, when properly understood, biblical doctrine can be seen for what it is—the lifeblood of an individual's knowledge of and relationship with God and His creation. Nothing we can ever study will have effects in our lives as far-reaching as our study of theology. So great can be its impact that Jesus Christ compared an understanding of its truths to being set free from slavery (John 8:31–32). Do you want to be free—to "mount up with wings like eagles" (Isa. 40:31) and to face the harsh realities of life with renewed strength and divine wisdom? Then get your backpack ready and put on your hiking gear. You are about to embark on the most important and life-changing climb you will ever make—the climb up the scenic slopes of Christian theology.

I. Ignorance Is Not Bliss

Something is happening to us today which has not happened for a very long time. We are waging a war of religion. Not a civil war between adherents of the same religion, but a life-and-death struggle between Christian and pagan.... At bottom it is a violent and irreconcilable quarrel about the nature of God and the nature of man and the ultimate nature of the universe; it is a war of dogma.[1]

Dorothy Sayers is right. Whether we want to face it or not, we *are* in a war of ideologies and world views virtually unprecedented since the first century A.D. Various forms of atheistic humanism declare

---

1. Dorothy L. Sayers, "Creed or Chaos?" in *The Necessity of Systematic Theology,* 2d ed., ed. John Jefferson Davis (Grand Rapids, Mich.: Baker Book House, 1978), p. 27.

that man must solve his own problems since there is no God to bail him out. Eastern gurus and masters claim to illumine the path of realization, showing us that we all are God, and that God is one with the universe. Mormon missionaries preach that we can become gods and populate our own planets if we will join their church and follow the teachings of their prophets. Wherever we turn, we find counterfeit gospels, non-Christian philosophies, and false messiahs—all striving to neutralize or debunk orthodox Christianity. How are Christians faring against all this? Sadly, not very well. Few believers today know what they believe or why they believe it. Theologically speaking, most Christians are ignorant of even the fundamentals of the faith. Consequently, they are prime targets of zealous non-Christians who wish to either destroy the faith of believers or win them over to a false belief system. Ignorance—especially doctrinal ignorance—is not bliss. It is the breeding ground for fear, prejudice, superstition, failure, and spiritual defeat. No wonder the Scriptures exhort us to learn the truth so well that we will "always [be] ready to make a defense to everyone who asks [us] to give an account for the hope that is in [us], yet with gentleness and reverence" (1 Pet. 3:15b). The word *defense* is a translation of the Greek term *apologia,* from which we get our words *apologetic* and *apology. Apologia,* however, is not the word one would use in Jesus' day to say "I'm sorry." Rather, the term carries the idea of giving a formal justification or convincing defense. And, according to the verse, what we are to always be ready to justify or defend is the hope within us—our faith in Christ. This ability requires a sound understanding of Christian doctrine coupled with a considerate, caring attitude and demeanor.

II. "Knowing the Scoop" Is Often Emphasized in Scripture

Although God reveals many truths through what He has made (Ps. 19:1–6; Acts 14:15–17; Rom. 1:18–20, 2:14–15), He has graciously chosen to clarify, expand on, and add to these truths in verbal and written form. For example, in the days of Moses, God etched the Ten Commandments on stone tablets for His people to learn and apply (Exod. 20:1–18, 31:18; Deut. 5:1–22). Before the Israelites marched into Canaan, God instructed Moses to pull them aside and deliver a series of sermons on the Law He had given, exhorting them to learn, obey, and teach it (see Deuteronomy, especially chap. 6). After the Hebrews had become settled in their new land, the prophet Samuel, according to God's desire, instituted a school of prophets that trained promising students to become spokesmen for the Lord (1 Sam. 19:20; compare 2 Kings 2:3, 5; 4:38; 6:1–2).[2] God continued to

2. See *Unger's Bible Dictionary,* rev. ed., by Merrill F. Unger (Chicago, Ill.: Moody Press, 1966), p. 891.

deliver His Word to the nation of Israel through a variety of other means, but none was more complete than the revelation He gave through His own Son, Jesus Christ (John 1:14–18, Heb. 1:1–2). Jesus fulfilled God's Word, taught from it, and continually directed people to learn and apply it (Matt. 5–7, 9:11–13, 15:1–20). The disciples who followed in Christ's steps established the Church on the Scriptures and frequently used them to defend the teachings of Christianity (Acts 7, 17:1–4, 18:24–28, 19:8–10). In fact, these pioneers of the faith exhorted all believers—church leaders and followers alike—to heed, teach, and defend Christian doctrine (Titus 1:7–9, Heb. 5:11–6:2, 1 Pet. 3:15, 1 John 5:1–3, Jude 3).[3] Such has been the Church's practice throughout her history.[4] From just this brief journey through the pages of the Bible, we can see that "as Christians we simply cannot avoid theology. We aren't all expected to be theologians in a technical or academic sense, but we are theologians with a small 't'. The question is not will we be theologians but will we be good theologians or poor theologians?"[5]

III. Six Benefits of Being Spiritually Informed

Now that we know how important it is to be well grounded in biblical doctrine, it might be good to see what we can gain by becoming theologically adept.

A. Knowledge gives substance to faith. Faith is trust. As we all know, before we place our trust in something, we need to have good reason to believe that it is trustworthy. Our knowledge informs us that it is unwise to sit in a chair that will collapse under our weight, or to fly in an airplane with a drunk pilot at the controls. Likewise, when we come to spiritual matters, we need to know in what or in whom we are being asked to trust before we decide to exercise our faith. No other criteria—be it emotion, human opinion, peer pressure, or tradition—is an adequate substitute for a working knowledge of Christian theology.

---

3. For more information on the use of apologetics in the New Testament, we would suggest consulting the following sources: *The Defense of the Gospel in the New Testament,* rev. ed., by F. F. Bruce (Grand Rapids, Mich.: William B. Eerdmans Publishing Co., 1977); *Challenge and Response: A Handbook of Christian Apologetics,* by Frederic R. Howe (Grand Rapids, Mich.: Zondervan Publishing House, 1982).

4. Some helpful sources on the history and variety of Christian apologetics are: *Classical Readings in Christian Apologetics: A.D. 100–1800,* ed. L. Russ Bush (Grand Rapids, Mich.: Academie Books, Zondervan Publishing House, 1983); *Varieties of Christian Apologetics,* by Bernard Ramm (Grand Rapids, Mich.: Baker Book House, 1976); *Testing Christianity's Truth-Claims: Approaches to Christian Apologetics,* by Gordon R. Lewis (Chicago, Ill.: Moody Press, 1976); *Christian Apologetics,* by Norman Geisler (Grand Rapids, Mich.: Baker Book House, 1976), chaps. 1–8.

5. R. C. Sproul, "Right Now Counts Forever," in *The Necessity of Systematic Theology,* p. 16.

B. Knowledge stabilizes us during times of testing.
Feelings fluctuate, moods change, and opinions vary. But biblical truth stands forever, giving us a foundation on which we can weather the storms of life (Matt. 7:24–25).

C. Knowledge enables us to handle the Bible accurately. A sound understanding of Christian doctrine will help us to interpret and apply God's Word intelligently, correctly, and wisely. Without a good foundation in theological knowledge, we run the risk of being like "children, tossed here and there by waves, and carried about by every wind of doctrine, by the trickery of men, by craftiness in deceitful scheming" (Eph. 4:14).

D. Knowledge equips us to detect and confront error.
The best way to detect a counterfeit bill is to learn what real money looks and feels like. Similarly, the most essential step in spotting and counteracting theological error is the gaining of a thorough knowledge of the truth.

E. Knowledge makes us confident in our daily walk with God. If we have a lot of ups and downs in our relationship to the Lord, it is likely due to an inconsistent intake of biblical nourishment—God's Word. The more we sit at His table and partake of His food, the stronger we will become in our spiritual lives.

F. Knowledge provides a grid that filters out our fears and superstitions. Ignorance is the well from which spring fear and superstition. An understanding of biblical theology helps us to dam up the flow of false teaching that threatens to drive us away from divine truth.

IV. A First-Century Example of the Value of Sound Doctrine

A clear biblical illustration of what we have learned so far can be found in the Apostle Paul's first letter to the young pastor Timothy. After citing a confessional creed that was commonly utilized in the early days of the Church (1 Tim. 3:16),[6] Paul informs Timothy about something "the Spirit explicitly says" (4:1a). The Greek term for *explicitly* means "expressly, clearly, unmistakably."[7] That is, the Holy Spirit has not shrouded this information in mystery or merely revealed a hint. The information He conveys is crystal clear and absolutely reliable. What is this statement of fact? "In later times some will fall away from the faith, paying attention to deceitful spirits and doctrines of demons" (v. 1b). The "later times" began during the

---

6. See *The Eucharistic Words of Jesus,* trans. Norman Perrin, by Joachim Jeremias (London: SCM Press, 1966), p. 102; and *The Earliest Christian Confessions,* by Vernon Neufeld (Grand Rapids, Mich.: William B. Eerdmans Publishing Co., 1964), pp. 7, 9, 128.

7. Fritz Rienecker, *A Linguistic Key to the Greek New Testament,* ed. Cleon L. Rogers, Jr. (Grand Rapids, Mich.: Zondervan Publishing House, 1980), p. 625.

earthly lifetime of Christ (Heb. 1:2, 1 Pet. 1:20). So Paul is saying that from Jesus' day until the final judgment of God (compare Matt. 13:36–43), some people will apostasize from, or abandon, the Christian faith. Why? Because they will heed the deceitful lies of individuals who may think they are teaching the truth but who in reality are drawing their doctrine from the pit of hell (1 Tim. 4:1–2). At the time Paul wrote this letter, the heresy that was beginning to threaten the Church was an incipient form of Gnosticism. Among the many beliefs in this religious system was the tenet that the material world was not created by God and that it is evil. From this understanding came the forbidding of marriage and the abstaining from certain kinds of food (v. 3a). Paul rightly condemned this heretical perspective by counteracting it with the truth: "Everything created by God is good, and nothing is to be rejected, if it is received with gratitude" (v. 4). Then Paul encouraged Timothy to refute Gnosticism before the Christian brethren under his care (v. 6a), constantly nourishing himself "on the words of the faith and of the sound doctrine" (v. 6b). How much we need to heed Paul's counsel in our own lives and churches!

V. Ten Major Areas of Doctrine

In this doctrinal series, we will zero in on ten key subjects of Christian theology: the Bible, God the Father, God the Son, God the Holy Spirit, the depravity of man, the salvation of man, the Second Advent of Christ, the Resurrection, the universal Church, and the local church. Within these topics reside the roots of Christianity. These areas are so important that we will briefly summarize them here in the form of a creedal statement each Christian should embrace without reservation.

—I affirm my confidence in God's inerrant Word. I treasure its truths and I respect its reproofs.

—I acknowledge the Creator-God as my heavenly Father, infinitely perfect, and intimately acquainted with all my ways.

—I claim Jesus Christ as my Lord—very God who came in human flesh—the object of my worship and the subject of my praise.

—I recognize the Holy Spirit as the third member of the Godhead, incessantly at work convicting, convincing, and comforting.

—I confess that Adam's fall into sin left humanity without the hope of heaven apart from a new birth, made possible by the Savior's death and bodily resurrection.

—I believe the offer of salvation is God's love-gift to all. Those who accept it by faith, apart from works, become new creatures in Christ.

—I anticipate my Lord's promised return, which could occur at any moment.

—I am convinced that all who have died will be brought back from beyond—believers to everlasting communion with God and unbelievers to everlasting separation from God.

—I know the Lord is continuing to enlarge His family, the universal Body of Christ, over which He rules as Head.

—I am grateful to be a part of a local church which exists to proclaim God's truth, to administer the ordinances, to stimulate growth toward maturity, and to bring glory to God.[8]

VI. Knowledge Alone Can Be Dangerous

As important as it is to learn doctrine, it would be dangerous for us to focus all our energy on this task alone. There are at least four dangers of which we should be aware.

A. Knowledge can be dangerous when it lacks intelligent, biblical support. Unless we sift all our knowledge through the grid of Scripture, we run a high risk of mixing error with truth, wrong with right.

B. Knowledge can be dangerous when it becomes an end in itself rather than a means to godliness. Knowledge alone tends to puff up our egos. But scriptural knowledge helps us become humble, transparent, and compassionate.

C. Knowledge can be dangerous when it isn't balanced by love and grace. Intolerance, divisiveness, arrogance—these are some of the rotten fruits we grow when we make gaining knowledge our only goal in life.

D. Knowledge can be dangerous when it remains theoretical—when it isn't mixed with discernment and action. Simply knowing what is true will not keep us from falling prey to temptation or false teachers. We need to consistently apply it to our lives if we are to experience genuine spiritual growth and strength.

VII. A Closing Thought to the Unconvinced

Perhaps you remain unmoved by what we have examined in this lesson. You may be saved, and you think that's all you need. "Besides," you reason, "I support ministers and missionaries to think for me. If they will just tell me what to believe, I'll believe it and get on with my life." Friend, if that's where you are, you need to seriously reflect on these words from Christ: " ' "You shall love the

8. Charles R. Swindoll, *Growing Deep in the Christian Life* (Portland, Oreg.: Multnomah Press, 1986), p. 15.

Lord your God with all your heart, and with all your soul, and *with all your mind.*" This is the great and foremost commandment'" (Matt. 22:37–38, emphasis added). If you really love the Lord, you will commit yourself to serving Him, not only with your heart and soul, but with your intellect as well. And that involves discovering, studying, and applying sound Christian doctrine. Not only will this help you grow in your faith, but it will make it possible for you to aid those who are weaker in the faith to stand firm against attack.

Living Insights

Study One

Is doctrine dull? No way! It is a fascinating study, full of interest and benefit for the student of Scripture. Let's begin our study with a pretest. Teachers use this tool to measure what their students already know about a particular subject. Under each heading below, write three to five statements based on what you already know from the Bible. If this is an easy test—great! If not, don't worry—you'll really profit as we continue our journey through the basics of the Christian faith.

What I Know about . . .

. . . the Bible _____

_____

_____

_____

_____

. . . God the Father _____

_____

_____

_____

_____

Continued on next page

... the Lord Jesus Christ _____

_____

_____

_____

_____

_____

... the Holy Spirit _____

_____

_____

_____

_____

_____

... the Depravity of Humanity _____

_____

_____

_____

_____

_____

Living Insights

Study Two

Now that we've completed the first half of the pretest, let's continue in the same vein. Make three to five succinct statements about each doctrine. As before, base your comments on information you already possess.

What I Know about . . .

... Salvation _____

_____

_____

_____

_____

. . . the Return of Christ _____

_____

_____

_____

_____

. . . the Resurrections of Christians and Non-Christians _____

_____

_____

_____

_____

. . . the Universal Church _____

_____

_____

_____

. . . the Local Church _____

_____

_____

_____

_____

Don't Forget to Add a Cup of Discernment

Selected Scripture

Knowledge is important. Without it, we could not grow intellectually, emotionally, morally, psychologically, or spiritually. However, knowledge *alone* can have a crippling effect on one's ability to grow. For example, knowledge that lacks love frequently becomes a source of pride. Knowledge without humility can lead to a judgmental attitude. And knowledge untempered by wisdom often spawns idealism and a perfectionistic spirit. There's no doubt about it—knowledge needs a companion, something to soften it, give it perspective, and make it realistic. What knowledge needs is *discernment.* Let's set our sights on this critical subject and spend some time discovering why we should mix discernment with our knowledge of Christian doctrine and how we can go about it.

I. Some Key Definitions

Before we go any farther, let's make sure we understand some crucial terms.

A. Knowledge. By *knowledge* we mean "the acquisition of biblical facts, principles, and doctrines." As such, knowledge involves a systematic understanding of Christian truth that assists us in accurately interpreting and applying the Scriptures. And although knowledge can bring about various emotions and lead to numerous actions, knowledge in and of itself lacks feelings and practical applications. Consequently, knowledge can remain on the theoretical plane of fact-gathering if we let it. And if we gain knowledge but do not utilize it in a loving way, it is worthless (1 Cor. 13:2). This is not to say that the accumulation of biblical data is unimportant. Christian theology is well worth understanding and defending (2 Cor. 10:5, Jude 3). However, it must be applied to life; otherwise, we abort its intended purpose and thereby render it fruitless (James 1:22–25, 2:19–20).

B. Discernment. "The ability to detect, to recognize, to perceive beyond what is said" is our definition of *discernment.* Put another way, discernment is the ability to sense something by means of intuition, to read between the lines, to have insight that goes beyond the obvious. It involves the ability to recognize evil, to sense goodness and truth, and to size up a situation or person accurately. As a political leader, King Solomon saw the great need he had for discernment. So he asked God to give it to him, and the Lord gladly did (1 Kings 3:6–12). In the realm of deciding whether something is true or not, the Apostle John commands us to exercise discernment by testing the truth-claims that come

10

our way (1 John 4:1–3). We are not to accept information as being true simply because someone says it is true. We are exhorted to check claims out, reason about them, and sift them through the grid of Scripture. Then, if they pass the appropriate tests, we should accept them as being true. Clearly, discernment is critical to the Christian life—important enough that the Apostle Paul made it a part of his prayer for the Philippian believers: "This I pray, that your love may abound still more and more in real knowledge and all discernment" (Phil. 1:9). How can we become discerning? It can't be taught—only caught or divinely bestowed. We need to seek it...pray for it...spend time with those who exercise it. As we mature in our knowledge and application of Christianity, we will grow in discernment (Heb. 5:11–14).

C. Balance. We understand the term *balance* to signify freedom from extremes. It includes the abilities to face life realistically and to consider contrary viewpoints with tolerance. Balanced Christians are those who maintain their spiritual equilibrium even in the presence of people who disagree with them. In short, the result of knowledge coupled with discernment is balance— the capacity to use information wisely.

II. Some Examples from Scripture

With these definitions firmly fixed in our minds, we are ready to consider some specific biblical illustrations of balance and extremism, knowledge wisely applied and knowledge foolishly abused. Let's look at two negative examples first, then focus on two positive illustrations.

A. Diotrephes—a leader out of line. The little letter of 3 John tells about a man who knew the truth but refused to submit himself to it. He allowed his love of authority and power to run roughshod over the church he attended. The Apostle John exposes and criticizes this individual in no uncertain terms:

> I wrote something to the church; but Diotrephes, who loves to be first among them, does not accept what we say. For this reason, if I come, I will call attention to his deeds which he does, unjustly accusing us with wicked words; and not satisfied with this, neither does he himself receive the brethren, and he forbids those who desire to do so, and puts them out of the church. Beloved, do not imitate what is evil, but what is good. The one who does good is of God; the one who does evil has not seen God. (3 John 9–11)

Diotrephes was out of control. His lack of discernment and willful abuse of his leadership position brought grief to those under his charge and discipline upon himself. We can fall into the same trap he did if we fail to guard ourselves against inflating our own importance. Perspective brought on by discernment will help us avoid this temptation of pride.

B. The Corinthian church—a contentious congregation. This was a first-century church that had all the knowledge and gifts it needed to mature spiritually (1 Cor. 1:4–7). And yet, as the Apostle Paul lamented, it was a body of people marked by quarrels and division (vv. 10–11). Apparently, there were "at least four factions, each having its own emphasis, following its own leader, and acting in antagonism to the other three."[1] The individuals these groups chose to rally around were Paul, Apollos, Cephas—otherwise known as Peter—and Christ (v. 12). Paul condemned the Corinthians' strife, calling it "fleshly" (3:3). And he suggested that their emphasis on knowledge alone had made them arrogant (8:1–2). What these Christians needed to balance their theology was a strong dose of discernment laced with a loving concern for the welfare of others (compare chaps. 8–9, 12–13). This would have helped them see where their extremism was leading them and how they could have corrected it. The same counsel holds true for us. We need to take stock of our lifestyle, weighing our words and actions to make sure they reflect biblical values and a caring heart.

C. Apollos—a preacher with a teachable spirit. Turning to Acts 18, we find a remarkable story about a minister who had it all together . . . almost, anyway. His name was Apollos. He was an Alexandrian Jew who knew the Old Testament well and believed that Jesus was the Messiah. Apparently, however, he knew little else about Christ and probably nothing about the baptism of the Holy Spirit, since he was only familiar with John's baptism of repentance (vv. 24–25; compare 19:1–6).[2] But armed with the knowledge he did have, Apollos spoke out fervently in the synagogue in Ephesus, proclaiming and defending the good news about Christ (18:24, 26a). When Priscilla and Aquila—a husband-and-wife missionary team trained by Paul (vv. 1–4, 18–21)[3]—heard Apollos speak, they recognized some deficiencies in his understanding of Christianity. So "they took him aside

---

1. W. Harold Mare, "1 Corinthians," in *The Expositor's Bible Commentary* (Grand Rapids, Mich.: Regency Reference Library, Zondervan Publishing House, 1976), vol. 10, p. 192.

2. See Richard N. Longenecker, "The Acts of the Apostles," in *The Expositor's Bible Commentary* (Grand Rapids, Mich.: Regency Reference Library, Zondervan Publishing House, 1981), vol. 9, pp. 490–91; and Stanley D. Toussaint, "Acts," in *The Bible Knowledge Commentary: New Testament Edition* (Wheaton, Ill.: Victor Books, 1983), pp. 408–9.

3. More information on Priscilla and Aquila and their relationship with Paul can be found in the study guide titled *A Family Album,* ed. Bill Watkins, from the Bible-teaching ministry of Charles R. Swindoll (Fullerton, Calif.: Insight for Living, 1984), pp. 6–8.

and explained to him the way of God more accurately" (v. 26b). How he must have soaked up what Priscilla and Aquila told him! For when he arrived in Achaia (v. 27), he used his new theological understanding to "powerfully [refute] the Jews in public, demonstrating by the Scriptures that Jesus was the Christ" (v. 28). His ability to discern what was true and to wisely apply it led to the opening of new evangelistic opportunities. Like Apollos, we must remain teachable if we want to be effective servants of Christ. And that involves the recognition that we are limited in our understanding of truth and that we can grow in our knowledge by learning from others.

D. The Berean synagogue—a perceptive body of Jews. After Paul and Silas had left Thessalonica, they came to a city called Berea (17:10a). Once there, "they went into the synagogue of the Jews" (v. 10b). The text indicates that the Berean Jews were much more open to the Christian message than were the Jews in Thessalonica: "Now [the Berean Jews] were more noble-minded than those in Thessalonica, for they received [that is, welcomed] the word with great eagerness, examining the Scriptures daily, to see whether these things were so" (v. 11). When they heard the gospel from Paul and Silas, they tested it against God's Word and found it to be consistent with what they knew to be true. So they embraced it unreservedly. But notice: the Berean Jews did not accept what they heard simply because some authoritative individuals had told them it was true. The Bereans heard Paul and Silas out, thought their message through, and compared it to the Scriptures. Once they were convinced that the Christian message was consistent with the other divine truth they knew, they believed in Christ and were saved (v. 12). Now that's an act of discernment that definitely had eternal ramifications! We, too, should carefully consider what others say, examining their teachings in light of God's Word.

III. Three Principles We Must Never Forget

Let's wrap up this study with some timeless principles that, when applied, can help guard us from becoming imbalanced in our acquisition of theological truth.

A. No one person has all the truth. Excluding the omniscient God, no individual knows everything. This realization should lead us to drink with discernment from the doctrinal wells of different persons and ministries—a practice that can protect us from spiritual stagnation and keep us from subsisting on bad theological water.

B. No single church owns exclusive rights to our minds. *Christ* is our Lord and Master, not some church, parachurch

13

ministry, or preacher (Eph. 1:20–23, 5:23–24). This fact should make us wary of any person or organization that attempts to dominate or control our thoughts.

C. No specific interpretation of Scripture is correct just because a gifted teacher says it is. The Berean Jews checked out what Paul and Silas said without any apparent flak from these missionaries. Their wise example should prompt us to check the claims and teachings of people today with the clearest standard of truth we have—the Bible.

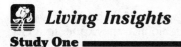 *Living Insights*

Study One ▬▬▬▬▬▬▬▬▬▬▬▬▬▬▬▬▬▬▬▬▬▬▬▬▬▬▬▬▬▬▬▬

In our study, we briefly referred to 1 John 4:1: "Beloved, do not believe every spirit, but test the spirits to see whether they are from God; because many false prophets have gone out into the world." This verse puts knowledge and discernment side by side. Let's probe further into this passage in order to discover how to test the spirits.

● Read 1 John 4. In that chapter you'll observe some significant truths. As you read it, keep this question in the front of your thinking: How can I test the spirits? You will find several answers in this chapter. Record your discoveries in this chart.

How Should I Test the Spirits?	
Verses	Methods of Discernment

14

Verses	Methods of Discernment

Living Insights

Study Two

The Bereans in Acts 17 are wonderful examples of discerning individuals. How discerning are you, my friend? Reflect on what we learned in this lesson, and take a few minutes to answer the following questions honestly.

- *No one person has all the truth.* Healthy Christians fill their diets with variety. How varied is your diet? Do you receive teaching from more than one human mouthpiece?

_____

_____

_____

_____

_____

Continued on next page

- *No single church owns exclusive rights to our minds.* Discerning Christians bow to *Christ's* lordship. Is your ultimate submission to Christ, or to a ministry? How does this battle reveal itself in your life?

  _____

  _____

  _____

  _____

  _____

- *No specific interpretation of Scripture is correct just because a gifted teacher says it is.* Balanced Christians continually study the Word. Do you look into the Scriptures for yourself? How reliant are you on gifted teachers?

  _____

  _____

  _____

  _____

  _____

God's Book—God's Voice
Psalm 119

To what or to whom do you turn when you are told you have cancer . . . when you unexpectedly lose your job . . . when a loved one dies suddenly . . . when your mate hands you divorce papers . . . when your unmarried teenage daughter tells you she is pregnant? Which lighthouse do you depend on to guide you safely through the storms of life? What is your refuge? Where do you find strength and comfort? One crutch people often lean on is *escapism.* Rather than face the loss or pain that confronts them, they deny its presence or simply run away from it. Another common response is *cynicism.* This flows from a preoccupation with struggles that festers into resentment, bitterness, and sometimes revenge. *Humanism* is yet another way to deal with problems. God's counsel is ignored, and human opinion and self-help aids are sought after and applied. A fourth common crutch—and, no doubt, the most dangerous one—is *occultism.* Mediums, witches, clairvoyants, fortune-tellers, card readers, astrologers—these are just a few of the demonic resources people turn to for answers and assistance in times of distress.

Are any of these four refuges really helpful? Do they supply the shelter and resources we need to help us handle life's demands, life's assaults, life's pains? Not in the long run. The only timelessly relevant and truly effective source of help is the Bible. It is God's Word to man—His infallible written guide for our lives. Let's take some time to explore this truth theologically and practically.

I. The Bible: The Absolutely Trustworthy Crutch

The Bible is the primary authority for our lives . . . the final resting place for our cares, worries, and griefs . . . the infallible resource in our questioning and search for truth. Without the secure foundation it provides, our lives would be wavering on the shifting ground of human thought and emotion. The necessity of God's book is clearly brought out in Psalm 119. There we read about a man who is enduring hard times, but is not relying on himself or other people to see him through. He is placing his hope for deliverance in God's Word (vv. 81–92). The psalmist knows that the Lord's Word is absolutely trustworthy. So, standing on the solid ground of the Scriptures, he waits for God to make good on His promises. We, too, can rely on what the Lord says. Indeed, His Word is the only crutch that will never fail us.

II. Why the Foundation Is So Dependable

What is it about the Bible that qualifies it as our foremost and final authority? The answer is found in the identity, inerrancy, and reliability of the Bible.

17

A. Its identity. The word *Bible* does not appear in Scripture at all. The term means "book," and it refers to the collection of sixty-six books that the people of God have historically accepted as the Word of God.[1] What does the Bible call itself? For an answer, let's look at several passages in the New Testament.

1. Luke 24:27, 32. After Jesus rose from the dead, He came to two disciples who were traveling toward the village of Emmaus (v. 13). As they walked together, Jesus, "beginning with Moses and with all the prophets, . . . explained to them the things concerning Himself in all the Scriptures" (v. 27). A while later, the two disciples remarked to each other, " 'Were not our hearts burning within us while He was speaking to us on the road, while He was explaining the Scriptures to us?' " (v. 32). The term "Scriptures" comes from the Greek word *graphē,* which means "that which is written." The Lord did not simply allow His message to be passed down orally from generation to generation. He recorded and preserved His message either personally or through human agents (Exod. 31:18, 34:27–28; Isa. 30:8–9; Jer. 30:1–2, 36:4). It was written in the language of the people, in words they could understand. In fact, the New Testament was composed in *Koinē* Greek—the everyday language of the vast majority of people that lived in the first-century Roman Empire.

2. John 17:14–17. These verses from John's Gospel are part of the longest recorded prayer of Jesus. Here He says to His heavenly Father:

> "I have given them Thy word; and the world has hated them, because they are not of the world, even as I am not of the world. I do not ask Thee to take them out of the world, but to keep them from the evil one. They are not of the world, even as I am not of the world. Sanctify them in the truth; Thy word is truth."

Just as God is truth (John 1:14, 14:6; Rom. 3:3–4), so is His Word (compare Ps. 119:142, 151, 160). Therefore, it has integrity and dependability on whatever matters it touches. Of

---

1. How the books of the Bible came to be accepted by believers as the writings of God while other religious materials did not is the basic issue surrounding canonicity. If you would like to probe this subject further, we would suggest you consult these sources: *From Ancient Tablets to Modern Translations: A General Introduction to the Bible,* by David Ewert (Grand Rapids, Mich.: Academie Books, Zondervan Publishing House, 1983); *A General Introduction to the Bible,* rev. ed., by Norman L. Geisler and William E. Nix (Chicago, Ill.: Moody Press, 1986); *Inspiration and Canonicity of the Bible,* by R. Laird Harris (Grand Rapids, Mich.: Zondervan Publishing House, 1969).

course, in our day truth is considered by many to be *relative*—that is, any given belief, teaching, or fact is thought to be true only for some people, at some places, and during some time periods. But the Bible purports to be true in an *absolute* sense. Its claims are true for *all* people, at *all* places, and at *all* times.[2] Now that's something we can trust in forever! And the Word, Jesus tells us, will make us free as we submit to it in our daily lives (John 8:31–32).

3. **First Thessalonians 2:13.** In his first letter to the Thessalonian Christians, Paul penned these insightful words: "We . . . constantly thank God that when you received from us the word of God's message, you accepted it not as the word of men, but for what it really is, the word of God, which also performs its work in you who believe." The Bible is *God's* Word. When we hear it or read it, we are receiving *His* message, listening to *His* voice, considering *His* thoughts. No other book on earth can legitimately make this claim.[3] The Bible as God's Word stands alone and above all other books in the world. We cannot find a more solid foundation to stand on or a more authoritative source to consult than Scripture.

4. **First Peter 1:23–25.** One more characteristic of the Bible is found in this text. Here Peter writes:

> You have been born again not of seed which is perishable but imperishable, that is, through the living and abiding word of God. For,
>> "All flesh is like grass,
>> And all its glory like the flower of
>>> grass.
>> The grass withers,
>> And the flower falls off,
>> But the Word of the Lord abides
>>> forever."
> And this is the word which was preached to you.

The Apostle affirms that God's Word is everlasting. Indeed, nothing else on earth will last forever except human beings. Everything else, including our material possessions, will be destroyed in a cosmic bonfire (2 Pet. 3:10). Realizing that fact should carry us a long way toward setting people and

2. It may be argued philosophically that *all* truth is absolute. Norman L. Geisler demonstrates this in his essay "Process Theology and Inerrancy," in *Challenges to Inerrancy: A Theological Response,* ed. Gordon R. Lewis and Bruce Demarest (Chicago, Ill.: Moody Press, 1984), p. 281.

3. Refutations of other claims to divine inspiration made by adherents of non-Christian religions may be found in Walter Martin's *The Kingdom of the Cults,* rev. ed. (Minneapolis, Minn.: Bethany House Publishers, 1985), and in Norman Geisler's *Christian Apologetics* (Grand Rapids, Mich.: Baker Book House, 1976), pp. 370–77.

our obedience to Scripture at the top of our priority list—above the accumulation of things or the pursuit of fame, power, or prestige.

B. Its inerrancy. We cannot gain a complete appreciation of the dependability of Scripture until we understand how God gave it to us—through imperfect, sinful beings like ourselves. To get a handle on this, let's become acquainted with three key terms and zero in on two central biblical passages.

1. **Terms to remember.** The giving of divine truth to man is referred to as *revelation*. This is the *fact* of God's communication to us, which occurs through three channels: creation, Christ, and the Bible (Rom. 1:18–20, Heb. 1:1–2, 2 Tim. 3:16). *Inspiration* occurred when the human writers received and recorded what God chose to reveal for that purpose. This was the *means* God chose to provide divine self-disclosure in written form, and it encompasses the Bible only. When we understand and apply God's truth correctly, we are experiencing *illumination*. This is a crucial *purpose* of divine communication which still takes place today. However, because the sixty-six books of the Bible stand as the completed written self-disclosure of God, revelation in written form—and inspiration, which is tied to it—have ceased.

2. **Passages to ponder.** When we think about God using sinful man to accurately record His Word, we can readily see that the most critical issue regarding this process is *inspiration*. Let's focus on this doctrine by considering two texts. The first one is 2 Timothy 3:16, which says in part, "All Scripture is inspired by God." The Greek words translated *inspired by God* literally mean "God-breathed." In other words, all the writings that comprise the Bible were breathed out by God. And notice: the doctrine of inspiration applies to the words of Scripture, not to the human writers. Moses, David, Luke, and Paul were not inspired to write Scripture like a composer may be inspired to write a song. Rather, God spoke through men like these, utilizing their individual personalities and styles to produce exactly the words He wanted to say. How did the Lord do this? Peter tells us: "No prophecy of Scripture is a matter of one's own interpretation, for no prophecy was ever made by an act of human will, but men *moved by the Holy Spirit* spoke from God" (2 Pet. 1:20–21, emphasis added). None of the human writers ever sat down and decided on their own to compose any of the books which make up the Bible. The human authors were moved by another—the Holy Spirit—who gave them the impetus and message

to write, and supervised the whole process. The result? Divinely authoritative writings that are without error in their original form. Theologian Paul Feinberg expresses the essence of *inerrancy* well: "Inerrancy means that when all facts are known the Scriptures in their original autographs and properly interpreted will be shown to be wholly true in everything they affirm, whether that has to do with doctrine or morality or with the social, physical, or life sciences."[4] Put another way, Scripture is what God has said infallibly through human agents. Therefore, we can have confidence that everything it says is true.

C. Its reliability. Because the Bible has been revealed and inspired by God—who is Himself truth, and thereby completely incapable of lying (Titus 1:2a)—it is absolutely reliable in all matters it deals with, be they spiritual, moral, psychological, historical, or scientific. No other book on earth can compare to this book. In fact, the Bible is the book by which all other claims to truth should be tested. Christian apologist Norman Geisler sums up the situation this way:

> Jesus is God incarnate. As God, whatever he teaches is true. . . . Jesus, who is God's full and final revelation, promised that his twelve apostles would be guided by the Holy Spirit into "all truth." The only authentic and confirmed record of apostolic teaching extant is the twenty-seven books of the New Testament. Hence, the canon of God's revelation to man is closed. With these sixty-six books we have the complete and final revelation of God for the faith and practice of believers. Every spirit or prophet who claims to give a new or different revelation is not of God.
>
> This does not mean that there is no truth in other religious writings or holy books. . . . The point is that the Bible and the Bible alone contains all doctrinal and ethical truth God has revealed to mankind. And the Bible alone is the canon or norm for all truth. All other alleged truth must be brought to the bar of Holy Scripture to be tested. The Bible and the Bible alone, all sixty-six books, has been confirmed by God through Christ to be his infallible Word.[5]

Now that's a book in which we can trust completely and unreservedly.

4. Paul D. Feinberg, "The Meaning of Inerrancy," in *Inerrancy,* ed. Norman L. Geisler (Grand Rapids, Mich.: Zondervan Publishing House, 1979), p. 294.

5. Geisler, *Christian Apologetics,* pp. 376–77.

III. Some Benefits of Relying on the Bible

Returning to Psalm 119, we discover at least three benefits we can enjoy by submitting our lives to God's Word.

A. Stability. Even when people rise up against us and events take a turn for the worse, we can find the counsel and strength we need in Scripture to stand firm (vv. 98, 110, 114–17). Are *you* relying on the Bible?

B. Insight. A deeper understanding of life will come from consistent meditation on God's Word (v. 99). Are *you* studying the Bible regularly?

C. Maturity. Our obedience to the Bible will result in maturity and wisdom that will surpass even those who are much older than we are (v. 100). Are *you* applying the timeless principles of Scripture to your life?

 Living Insights

Study One

The longest chapter in the Bible is Psalm 119. It is a psalm dedicated to the supreme authority of the Word of God.

- As we read through Psalm 119, we can observe the writer facing most of life's major battles. Yet with each battle, he reaffirms the reliability of God's Word and returns to it for counsel. Using the charts on the following two pages, work your way through as much of this psalm as your study time permits.

Relying on God's Word—Psalm 119	
Life's Major Battles	
Verses	Observations

Continued on next page

Relying on God's Word—Psalm 119	
Description of God's Word	
Verses	Observations

🔖 *Living Insights*

Has the Bible been your source of strength in the past? Let's do a little personal inventory on this subject.

How would you rate your personal Bible study?

Excellent   Good   OK   Poor   Completely absent

Reason for your rating:

How involved are you in small group Bible study?

Very involved   Somewhat involved   Uninvolved

Reason for your rating:

How would you rate your overall dependence on God's Word?

Couldn't be better   Good   OK   Poor   Completely absent

Reason for your rating:

If you were weak in any of these areas, take this opportunity to devise and initiate a plan that will help you grow more dependent on God through His Word. The benefits you will gain will far outweigh any cost you may need to pay.

Handling the Scriptures Accurately

Matthew 9, 12, 15, 16; Nehemiah 8

We often hear about and sometimes experience abuse. The abuse may be sexual, emotional, or verbal, but in every case it leaves its scars on those who feel the brunt of its blows. There is one kind of abuse, however, that doesn't receive the critical attention it deserves, and that's *abuse of the Bible.*[1] Many, if not all, of us have witnessed someone twisting Scripture, forcing a meaning onto a passage to make it say something other than what it actually says. Sometimes this is done unknowingly. Other times, however, it is done with malice and deception. But in either case, the result is frequently the same—other people walk away thinking that the Bible teaches something it does not. And if these people embrace the faulty interpretation or application, they run the risk of harming at least their own spiritual health and growth, and possibly that of others. That is the ultimate rip-off, and it has serious ramifications.

Unfortunately, Scripture twisters are not always easy to spot. They usually are not outright con artists or individuals who are struggling to gain a hearing for their views. Many Bible abusers are sincere, personable, popular, and even theologically knowledgeable. Some of them may even live in our homes and wear our clothes. We need to learn how to handle God's Word accurately so that we can (1) avoid engaging in and falling victim to Bible abuse and (2) become more mature in our walk with God. In this lesson we will explore this subject and consider some practical steps we can take toward becoming better interpreters of the Scriptures.

I. Our Need: Maintaining the Meaning

Although Bible abuse is common today, it is not new: it has been around for a very long time. In Jesus' day, some of the most serious Scripture twisting came from the professional clergy—the Pharisees, the Sadducees, and the scribes. These were men devoted to the preservation and proclamation of Scripture. But in their attempts to interpret the Word, they often mishandled it. On several occasions Jesus Christ confronted them on this issue, each time making it clear that their need—like ours—was to discover and apply the correct meaning of God's Word. Let's turn the pages of Scripture to the Gospel of Matthew and take a look at some of these confrontations.

A. Matthew 9:9–13. While attending a banquet at Matthew's house, Jesus' disciples were approached by some Pharisees who

---

1. An excellent exception is James Sire's *Scripture Twisting: 20 Ways the Cults Misread the Bible* (Downers Grove, Ill.: InterVarsity Press, 1980).

were upset that Jesus was dining with "tax-gatherers and sinners" (vv. 9–11; compare Luke 5:29–30). The Jews despised tax collectors because "they collected money to support the Romans, and . . . often took in more than necessary and pocketed the difference."[2] The "sinners" were likely the "common folk who did not share all the scruples of the Pharisees. . . . [The designation] almost certainly . . . groups together those who broke Pharisaic Halakoth (rules of conduct)—harlots, tax collectors, and other disreputable people."[3] When Jesus heard the self-righteous Pharisees ask His disciples why He was eating with the "dregs of society," He told them,

> "It is not those who are healthy who need a physician, but those who are sick. But go and learn what this means, 'I desire compassion, and not sacrifice,' for I did not come to call the righteous, but sinners." (Matt. 9:12–13)

Commenting on this passage, New Testament scholar D. A. Carson writes:

> The quotation (v. 13) is from Hosea 6:6 and is introduced by the rabbinic formula "go and learn," used of those who needed to study the text further. Use of the formula may be slightly sardonic: those who prided themselves in their knowledge of and conformity to Scripture needed to "go and learn" what it means.[4]

B. Matthew 12:1–8. At another time, the Pharisees spotted Jesus and His disciples picking and eating grain on the Sabbath (vv. 1–2a). This act brought charges of lawbreaking from the Pharisees (v. 2b); for, according to their rule book, Halakah, picking grain on the Sabbath was not permitted except "in the case of temple service and where life was at stake."[5] Since neither exception applied in this instance, they thought they had trapped Jesus and His followers. But Jesus laid the charges to rest with three arguments, each of which were grounded in God's Word:

> "[1] Have you not read what David did, when he became hungry, he and his companions; how he

---

2. Louis A. Barbieri, "Matthew," in *The Bible Knowledge Commentary: New Testament Edition*, ed. John F. Walvoord and Roy B. Zuck (Wheaton, Ill.: Victor Books, 1983), p. 39.

3. D. A. Carson, "Matthew," in *The Expositor's Bible Commentary* (Grand Rapids, Mich.: Regency Reference Library, Zondervan Publishing House, 1984), vol. 8, p. 224.

4. Carson, "Matthew," p. 225.

5. Carson, "Matthew," p. 280.

entered the house of God, and they ate the conse-
crated bread, which was not lawful for him to eat,
nor for those with him, but for the priests alone?
[2] Or have you not read in the Law, that on the
Sabbath the priests in the temple break the Sabbath,
and are innocent? [3] But I say to you, that something
greater than the temple is here. But if you had known
what this means, 'I desire compassion, and not a sacrifice,' you would not have condemned the innocent.
For the Son of Man is Lord of the Sabbath." (vv. 3–8)

C. Matthew 15:1–14. Later, a group of Pharisees and scribes
questioned Jesus concerning the disciples' failure to wash their
hands before eating bread (vv. 1–2). This act of omission was
viewed by these religious authorities as a violation of their traditional rules of conduct (compare Mark 7:3–4).[6] Jesus countered
their attack by showing them that they were guilty of breaking
God's law for the sake of keeping man-made laws (Matt. 15:3–6).
After He had exposed and condemned the hypocrisy of these
religious leaders (vv. 7–11), the disciples came to Jesus and
asked Him if He realized that He had made the Pharisees angry
(v. 12). Jesus' strong reply made it clear that He had no tolerance
for those hypocrites and their misuse of Scripture (vv. 13–14).

D. Matthew 16:5–12. This passage illustrates a problem different from the ones we have examined so far. In the previous passages, some of the *teachers* of God's Word were found guilty of
twisting or misunderstanding its meaning. However, in Matthew 16,
Christ speaks, and His *hearers* fail to grasp His meaning. After
Jesus, on two occasions, had fed thousands of people by miracu-
lously multiplying a little food into an abundant feast (14:13–21,
15:32–38), He warned His disciples, " 'Watch out and beware of
the leaven of the Pharisees and the Sadducees' " (16:6). The disciples thought that the warning was made because they hadn't
brought any bread with them (v. 7). So Jesus made it clear to
them that He was not warning them about literal bread but
about the teaching of the Pharisees and Sadducees (vv. 8–12).
Because the disciples had not paid close enough attention to
Jesus' use of words, they had misunderstood Him. Similarly, the
misinterpretation and misapplication of the Bible often involves
the same error. We need to be students of words in our study
of Scripture, probing for their meaning until we understand the
message of the passage in which they are found.

6. See Carson, "Matthew," p. 348.

II. An Example: Ezra and the Scroll

Looking to the Old Testament, we can see in Nehemiah 8 a prime example of God's Word being handled accurately and respectfully. After rebuilding the wall around Jerusalem (Neh. 1–6), the Hebrews "gathered as one man at the square which was in front of the Water Gate, and they asked Ezra the scribe to bring the book of the law of Moses which the Lord had given to Israel" (8:1). Ezra did as the people asked, then stepped up to "a wooden podium which they had made for the purpose [of reading the Law]" (v. 4). From the events that transpired, we can make at least four observations regarding the accurate use of God's Word.

A. Accurately handling the Scriptures starts with reading the Scriptures. Standing behind the podium situated above the people, Ezra read from the Mosaic Law (vv. 3–5). The Hebrews "were attentive to the book of the law" (v. 3b), regarding it as God's message to them. Likewise, we need to read the Scriptures, both silently and aloud, allowing the Lord to speak to us through His written Word.

B. Accurately handling the Scriptures includes having respect for the Scriptures. By constructing a podium for the reading of Scripture and placing it so that it stood above the people, the Jews were indicating their belief that God's Word had authority over their lives. A further expression of their reverence for Scripture occurred when they stood up "from early morning until midday" as it was read to them (vv. 3, 5). Finally, their submissive response to God and His Word is revealed in verse 6: "Then Ezra blessed the Lord the great God. And all the people answered, 'Amen, Amen!' while lifting up their hands; then they bowed low and worshiped the Lord with their faces to the ground." Although they did not worship Scripture, the Jews realized that they could not be faithful servants of God without submitting to the authority of His Word. So it is with us. The level of our honor and love for the Lord will be indicated by the degree to which we respect and conform to His Book (compare John 14:15, 1 John 2:3–6).

C. Accurately handling the Scriptures means that the truth is explained so that all can understand. As the Mosaic Law was read, interpreters were present, "translating to give the sense so that [the Jews] understood the reading" (Neh. 8:8). The Hebrew word for *translating* means "to make distinct, to separate." In verse 8, the term conveys the idea of taking something apart so as to make it clear and understandable. The Hebrew word rendered *sense* amplifies this definition, since it expresses the thought of shedding light on something which otherwise is unclear. These Jews needed to have the Hebrew Scriptures explained to them because they were fresh from seventy years of captivity in Babylonia. There they had learned to use a foreign language, to think with a Babylonian mind-set, and to live in a pagan culture. Therefore, the Jews had linguistic, intellectual, and cultural barriers that had to be crossed before genuine communication of God's Word could occur. Today, we have these same barriers to cross. Thus, we need to sit under teachers and read books that can build bridges of understanding from the Bible's original setting to our contemporary situation.

D. Accurately handling the Scriptures results in obedience to the Scriptures. Following the reading and interpreting of the Law, the Hebrews "went away to eat, to drink, to send portions and to celebrate a great festival, because they understood the words which had been made known to them" (v. 12; compare vv. 13–18). Their response to hearing God's voice through His Word was obedience. Likewise, when we understand what God says, we should heed it.

III. Tools for the Trade

The proper interpretation and application of God's Word requires the use of certain Bible study aids. At minimum, a serious student of the Scriptures should have a Bible concordance, a Bible dictionary, a Bible atlas, and some Bible commentaries. The acquisition of these tools involves some financial investment, but the cost pales into insignificance when you consider the gains that can come with a clear understanding of Scripture.

IV. Some Counsel to Victims of Bible Abuse

People who have been influenced by Bible abusers tend to become Bible abusers themselves. If you have been hurt in this way, don't channel your anger into harming others in a similar fashion. Forgive those who led you astray, abandon their teachings, and commit yourself to a lifelong pursuit of absorbing and applying the real truths of the Bible. You and those you come in contact with will be the better for it.

V. Rules to Remember

How can we avoid becoming Bible abusers? What can we do to help ensure that we will handle the Scriptures correctly? Our adherence to these five simple rules will help immensely.

A. Never forget *what* you are handling. The Bible is *God's* book. Recalling this fact will keep us sensitive.

B. Always remember *who* has the authority. The divine Author of Scripture has the ultimate authority over our lives, and He has commanded us to obey His Word. This fact should make us humble.

C. Keep in mind *why* you are teaching. The purpose for teaching the Bible is not to impress others with our knowledge or to cram our hobbyhorses down our audience's throat. Rather, the goal of Bible instruction—and Bible study—is to capture the original meaning of the text and to accurately explain and apply it so that it is meaningful for today.

D. Think about *where* people are. People come from different backgrounds, locales, professions, and home situations. Keeping this in mind will help us communicate the message of Scripture in an interesting and relevant way.

E. Focus on *when* the teaching ends. Once we have learned what the text says, we need to deal with its application in our lives. Only when Scripture is applied does it fulfill its whole purpose in the plan of God. And only when the Lord's Word is fitted with shoe leather in our lives do we begin to reap the fullness of the benefits it has to offer.

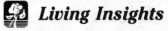 *Living Insights*

Study One ━━━━━━━━━━━━━━━━━━━━━━━━━━━━━━━━━━━━━━━

Discovering the original meaning of the passage is critical in our study of Scripture. Let's observe how this task of interpretation affects the results of inductive Bible study.

● Reread Nehemiah 8 and answer the question, What does this passage say? This step is called *observation*.

Observation: What does it say?

Continued on next page

- Next, answer the question, What does it mean? This is called *interpretation*.

Interpretation: What does it mean?

- Conclude with the question, How does it apply to me? This is *application*—the last leg of the Bible study process.

Application: How does it apply to me?

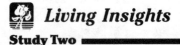

Living Insights

If you are serious about personal Bible study, you'll need to get your hands on some tools that will aid you in the study process. Use this Living Insights to do a little inventory of your bookshelves.

- Do I have a Bible concordance? _____
  Is it exhaustive? _____
  Is it compatible to the version of the Bible that I use? _____

- What do I have in the way of a Bible dictionary? _____
  Is it reasonably current? _____
- Do I have use of a Bible atlas? _____
  Am I relying only on the maps at the back of my Bible? _____
  Are they sufficient for the level of my study? _____
- Do I have a one-volume commentary on the whole Bible? _____
  Do I have commentaries for the individual books? _____

⚒ Digging Deeper

Choosing Bible study aids that are helpful to you can sometimes be a difficult and confusing task. In order to simplify the process, we have provided a list of some of the basic study tools we think are particularly informative and relatively easy to use. Of course, you must be the final judge of a book's usefulness for you. But we would suggest that you begin your search for just the right Bible aids with the following books.

• Biblical Interpretation
Barber, Cyril J. *Dynamic Personal Bible Study.* Foreword by Charles C. Ryrie. Neptune, N.J.: Loizeaux Brothers, 1981.

Fee, Gordon D., and Douglas Stuart. *How to Read the Bible for All Its Worth: A Guide to Understanding the Bible.* Grand Rapids, Mich.: Academie Books, Zondervan Publishing House, 1982.

Mickelsen, A. Berkeley, and Alvera M. Mickelsen. *Understanding Scripture: A Laymen's Guide to Interpreting the Bible.* Ventura, Calif.: Regal Books, 1982.

Sterrett, T. Norton. *How to Understand Your Bible.* Revised edition. Downers Grove, Ill.: InterVarsity Press, 1974.

Vos, Howard F. *Effective Bible Study: A Guide to Sixteen Methods.* Grand Rapids, Mich.: Zondervan Publishing House, 1956.

Wald, Oletta. *The Joy of Discovery in Bible Study.* Revised edition. Minneapolis, Minn.: Augsburg Publishing House, 1975.

• Bible Concordances
You should select a concordance based on the translation of the Bible you use. With this in mind, concordances have been listed for several versions.

The Complete Concordance to the Bible: New King James Version. Nashville, Tenn.: Thomas Nelson Publishers, 1983.

Goodrick, Edward W., and John R. Kohlenberger III. *The NIV Complete Concordance.* Grand Rapids, Mich.: Zondervan Publishing House, 1981. For the New International Version.

Nelson's Complete Concordance of the Revised Standard Version Bible. 2d ed. Nashville, Tenn.: Thomas Nelson Publishers, 1978.

New American Standard Exhaustive Concordance of the Bible.
Nashville, Tenn.: Holman Bible Publishers, 1981.

Strong, James. *The New Strong's Exhaustive Concordance of the Bible.* Nashville, Tenn.: Thomas Nelson Publishers, 1984. For the King James Version.

• **Dictionaries and Encyclopedias**

Alexander, Pat. *The Lion Encyclopedia of the Bible.* Revised edition. Batavia, Ill.: Lion Publishing Corp., 1986.

The Illustrated Bible Dictionary. 3 vols. Wheaton, Ill.: Tyndale House Publishers, 1984. This set is an illustrated version of the *New Bible Dictionary,* Wheaton, Ill.: Tyndale House Publishers, 1982.

The International Standard Bible Encyclopedia. 4 vols. Revised edition. Grand Rapids, Mich.: William B. Eerdmans Publishing Co., 1979– .

Unger, Merrill F. *Unger's Bible Dictionary.* 3d ed. Chicago, Ill.: Moody Press, 1966.

The Zondervan Pictorial Encyclopedia of the Bible. 5 vols. Grand Rapids, Mich.: Regency Reference Library, Zondervan Publishing House, 1976.

• **Atlases, Almanacs, and Archaeology Books**

Aharoni, Yohanan, and Michael Avi-Yonah. *The Macmillan Bible Atlas.* Revised edition. New York, N.Y.: Macmillan Publishing Co.; London: Collier Macmillan Publishers, 1977.

Avigad, Nahman. *Discovering Jerusalem.* Nashville, Tenn.: Thomas Nelson Publishers, 1980.

Beitzel, Barry J. *The Moody Atlas of Bible Lands.* Chicago, Ill.: Moody Press, 1985.

Bruce, F. F. *Abraham and David: Places They Knew.* Nashville, Tenn.: Thomas Nelson Publishers, 1984.

————. *Jesus and Paul: Places They Knew.* Nashville, Tenn.: Thomas Nelson Publishers, 1981.

Jenkins, Simon. *Bible Mapbook.* Belleville, Mich.: Lion Publishing Corp., 1985.

Mackowski, Richard M. *Jerusalem, City of Jesus.* Grand Rapids, Mich.: William B. Eerdmans Publishing Co., 1980.

May, Herbert G., ed. *Oxford Bible Atlas.* New York, N.Y.: Oxford University Press, 1974.

Millard, Alan. *Treasures from Bible Times.* Belleville, Mich.: Lion Publishing Corp., 1985.

Negev, Avraham, ed. *The Archaeological Encyclopedia of the Holy Land.* Revised edition. Nashville, Tenn.: Thomas Nelson Publishers, 1986.

The New International Dictionary of Biblical Archaeology. Grand Rapids, Mich.: Regency Reference Library, Zondervan Publishing House, 1983.

Packer, James I., Merrill C. Tenney, and William White, Jr., eds. *The Bible Almanac.* Nashville, Tenn.: Thomas Nelson Publishers, 1980.

Vos, Howard F. *Archaeology in Bible Lands.* Chicago, Ill.: Moody Press, 1977.

- **Commentaries**

Bible Student's Commentary. Grand Rapids, Mich.: Regency Reference Library, Zondervan Publishing House, 1981–   .

Bruce, F. F., ed. *International Bible Commentary.* Grand Rapids, Mich.: Zondervan Publishing House, 1986.

The Expositor's Bible Commentary. 12 vols. Grand Rapids, Mich.: Regency Reference Library, Zondervan Publishing House, 1978–   .

Motyer, J. A., and John R. W. Stott, eds. *The Bible Speaks Today Series.* Downers Grove, Ill.: InterVarsity Press, 1974–   .

Tyndale New Testament Commentaries. 20 vols. Grand Rapids, Mich.: William B. Eerdmans Publishing Co., 1957–71.

Tyndale Old Testament Commentaries. 18 vols. Downers Grove, Ill.: InterVarsity Press, 1968–   .

Walvoord, John F., and Roy B. Zuck, eds. *The Bible Knowledge Commentary.* 2 vols. Wheaton, Ill.: Victor Books, 1983, 1985.

Knowing God:
Life's Major Pursuit
Jeremiah 9:23–24, 29:11–14

"Win through intimidation" . . . "Get in touch with yourself" . . . "The goal of life is to know and love yourself" . . . "Look out for number one." We are a society obsessed with self. We do all we can to please ourselves, exalt ourselves, groom ourselves, protect ourselves, advance ourselves, and motivate ourselves. Our self-oriented pursuits are telltale signs that we are infected with man's most deadly disease—*me-ism.* In one hand, me-ism holds out the promise of fame, fortune, power, and a full understanding of self. But with the other hand, me-ism delivers hollowness, loneliness, self-destructive greed, and a greatly distorted picture of self.

The fact is, we will never find true success or the truth about ourselves until we start taking regular doses of the cure for this disease—*the pursuit of the knowledge of God.* Do you want to understand yourself, find lasting contentment, and accumulate riches that can never be taken from you? Then you must get your eyes off yourself and fix them on the Lord. Until you do, all your pursuits will be as dead-end streets—going nowhere.

I. The Wail of a Weeping Prophet

The prophet Jeremiah understood the value of making the knowledge of God life's major pursuit. More than two thousand years ago, Jeremiah was serving the Lord in a nation gone awry. Although the people knew God's Law, they had turned from Him to worship false gods and to pursue a life of self-indulgence. Consequently, they were destroying themselves and bringing divine judgment upon their land. Jeremiah wept over the Hebrews' spiritual obstinance and imminent demise (Jer. 8:13–9:1). But at the same time, he wished that he was miles away from his people because of their extreme wickedness (9:2–3). Why were the Israelites so sinful? What was the foundational cause of their disease? The Lord supplies the answer: " 'They do not know Me' " (v. 3b). Rather than seek God and conform their lives to His Word, the Hebrews chose to make self their central focus. This led to their adoption of a counterfeit value system—one that leaned on and exalted human wisdom, human might, and human wealth. The way back to personal and national health for the Israelites involved their taking a simple prescription as given by the divine Physician:

> Thus says the Lord, "Let not a wise man boast of his wisdom, and let not the mighty man boast of his might, let not a rich man boast of his riches; but let him who boasts boast of this, *that he understands and knows Me,*

that I am the Lord who exercises lovingkindness, justice,
and righteousness on earth; for I delight in these things,"
declares the Lord. (vv. 23–24, emphasis added)

The original Hebrew term for *understand* means "to have correct insight into the nature of an object." It includes the idea of conducting oneself wisely and dealing prudently with others. When this word is used in relation to the Lord, it conveys the thought of "conforming one's life to the character of God."[1] The Hebrew term translated *knows* refers to knowledge gained by the senses, not to knowledge acquired purely by rational thought. This word also speaks of the possession of an intimate acquaintance with someone.[2] Put another way, a person who knows God is an individual who knows Him as a friend knows a friend, or even as a lover knows a loved one. And because the object of his knowledge is the Lord of the universe, he bows before God in humble obedience and adoration. When these two terms are linked together, the cure for me-ism in any generation becomes even clearer: all the powers and faculties of a human being must be centered on and subjected to the living God (compare Matt. 22:36–37). We must, as far as we are capable, see ourselves as He sees us, understand life as He understands it, view our circumstances and those around us through the lens of His sovereign plan.

II. The Importance of Knowing God

"The highest science, the loftiest speculation, the mightiest philosophy, which can ever engage the attention of a child of God, is the name, the nature, the person, the work, the doings, and the existence of the great God whom he calls his Father."[3] But because God is infinite, it is absolutely impossible for us to arrive at a complete understanding of Him and His activities. Therefore, we will spend our time in the remainder of this lesson not trying to explain God's nature, but attempting to develop a thirst for drinking at His inexhaustible, thoroughly refreshing well. Before we do so, however, we should underscore the fact that through creation, history, and even our own consciences, we have sufficient evidence that God exists and that He deserves our worship and obedience (Ps. 19:1–6; Acts 14:16–17; Rom. 1:18–23, 2:14–16). This evidence is so compelling that children actually have to be taught to disbelieve in a deity.[4] Realizing how far

1. *Theological Wordbook of the Old Testament,* ed. R. Laird Harris (Chicago, Ill.: Moody Press, 1980), vol. 2, p. 877.

2. *Theological Wordbook,* ed. Harris, vol. 1, p. 366.

3. C. H. Spurgeon, as quoted by J. I. Packer in *Knowing God* (Downers Grove, Ill.: InterVarsity Press, 1973), p. 13.

4. An interesting support of this statement is the fact that an atheist has written a book to guide children toward embracing atheism. The book is *What about Gods?* by Chris Brockman (Buffalo, N.Y.: Prometheus Books, 1978).

God has gone to reveal Himself to us, let's concentrate on why it is important to pursue an intimate understanding of Him.

A. **Knowing God gives us the desire to be like Him.** When the Lord refers to Himself in Scripture, He almost always specifies some of His character traits. And when He does this, He frequently implies or even outright commands that His people model themselves after His moral attributes and example. An excellent illustration of this is found in 1 Peter 1:14–16, which reads: "As obedient children, do not be conformed to the former lusts which were yours in your ignorance, but like the Holy One who called you, be holy yourselves also in all your behavior; because it is written, 'You shall be holy, for I am holy.' " Just as our earthly parents want us to emulate the best in them, so our heavenly Father, who is perfect, desires us to become like Him in every way that we possibly can (compare Matt. 5:48). And as we get to know Him, our hunger will grow all the more to know Him even better and to conform ourselves to Him.

B. **Knowing God reveals the truth about ourselves.** A clear picture of this principle can be seen in the opening pages of the prophet Isaiah's book. In the sixth chapter, we see a snapshot of six six-winged angels singing praises to the Lord while He is "sitting on a throne, lofty and exalted, with the train of His robe filling the temple" (vv. 1–3). As Isaiah sees this vision, he cries out, " 'Woe is me, for I am ruined! / Because I am a man of unclean lips, / And I live among a people of unclean lips; / For my eyes have seen the King, the Lord of hosts' " (v. 5). Encountering the Lord helps us to gain a better understanding of ourselves. When we come to terms with His holiness, His patience, and His strength, we really begin to see our sinfulness, our impatience, and our weakness. And once we have an accurate appraisal of ourselves, our knowledge of God will direct us to the one who has the power and desire to meet our needs in the best way achievable (Matt. 6:25–33, Rom. 8:28–30).

C. **Knowing God enables us to interpret our world properly.** The Babylonian king Nebuchadnezzar learned the validity of this truth in a very dramatic way. During the height of his rule, Nebuchadnezzar became conceited. Rather than crediting God with his success, he praised himself (Dan. 4:28–30). The Lord responded to Nebuchadnezzar's arrogance by causing him to go insane. The monarch became like a wild beast for seven years (vv. 31–33; compare vv. 24–25). At the end of that time, God restored the king's ability to reason (v. 34a). Realizing what had happened to him and why, Nebuchadnezzar praised the Lord, exalting God's everlasting sovereignty over creation (vv. 34b–35).

Likewise, when we come to know God for who He is, our perspective changes. We begin to see the world as He does, and we start to realize that He is in control of all things—including us and our circumstances.

D. Knowing God makes us stronger and more secure. In the midst of a prophecy concerning Israel and her fight against foreign rule and religious oppression, we find this relevant truth: " 'By smooth words he will turn to godlessness those who act wickedly toward the covenant, but the people who know their God will display strength and take action' " (11:32). Those who depend on God—the God of Scripture—find a source of power that enables them to withstand even the most vicious and unrelenting attacks on their faith.

E. Knowing God introduces us to the eternal dimension of existence. Praying to His Father in heaven, Jesus said, " 'This is eternal life, that they may know Thee, the only true God, and Jesus Christ whom Thou has sent' " (John 17:3). If we know who God is, we will recognize His Son when we are introduced to Him. And if we have believed in the Father, we will believe in the Son and thereby become adopted children of God's everlasting family. Once we enter the community of the saved, we become inheritors of His invisible, indestructible, and eternal kingdom (18:36; 1 Cor. 2:9, 15:50; Gal. 3:26–4:31; Heb. 12:28; 2 Pet. 1:10–11). This change of citizenship brings with it a perspective that begins to lift our minds above the temporal and renew them with the eternal. In other words, a knowledge of God and a saving relationship with Him makes us heavenly-minded so that we can truly be of earthly good. As C. S. Lewis has said:

> If you read history you will find that the Christians who did most for the present world were just those who thought most of the next. The Apostles themselves, who set on foot the conversion of the Roman Empire, the great men who built up the Middle Ages, the English Evangelicals who abolished the Slave Trade, all left their mark on Earth, precisely because their minds were occupied with Heaven. It is since Christians have largely ceased to think of the other world that they have become so ineffective in this. Aim at Heaven and you will get earth "thrown in": aim at earth and you will get neither.[5]

5. C. S. Lewis, *Mere Christianity* (New York, N.Y.: Macmillan Publishing Co., 1952), p. 118.

III. The Presence of Incomprehensible Subjects

As important as knowing God is, it is impossible for us to know Him fully. After all, He is unlimited in all that He is, while we are limited in every way. Therefore, we will never have God completely figured out. Some aspects of Him and His dealings will always be mysterious to us. This fact should lead us to praise God, as it did the Apostle Paul (Rom. 11:33). For some of us, however, these unsolvable enigmas have prompted us to abandon the reasonableness of Christianity. This is terribly unfortunate. Although orthodox Christianity does contain some elements that go *beyond* reason, it does *not* teach anything that goes *against* reason. God is eminently rational, and He commands His people to avoid "opposing arguments" (1 Tim. 6:20)—literally, antitheses or contradictions. Therefore, we are *morally obligated* to accept the incomprehensible in Christianity without abandoning the reasonableness of Christianity.[6] Among the mysteries in Christianity we could mention, four are especially pertinent to our discussion on God.

A. Trinity. According to this doctrine, God is one in essence but three in personhood. Put another way, there are three coequal, coeternal, coexistent persons who have the same divine nature. They are not three separate gods, but one God existing in three distinct persons—God the Father, God the Son, and God the Holy Spirit. Exactly how they exist in one nature and specifically how they relate to one another are two of the subjects that seem to be partially unsolvable.

B. Glory. Moving from the triune *personhood* of God, we come to the *presence* of God—His glory. Divine glory concerns the luminous manifestation of the Lord's person in creation and history (2 Chron. 7:1–3, Ps. 19:1).[7] How the Lord reveals His personal presence without entering into time and space in His essence is a deep mystery.

C. Sovereignty. The biblical teaching on divine sovereignty concerns the *plan* of God. He is certainly in control of what goes on in the universe (Job 12:23–24, Ps. 65:9–10, Dan. 4:17, Matt. 6:26–31, Acts 17:25–27, Rom. 8:28). And yet, He does not manipulate or force free creatures to act in opposition to their wills (Gen. 3, Matt. 23:37, Acts 2:22–23). The Lord is not a cosmic puppeteer and we His puppets. Somehow, He holds the reins on creation

---

6. A more complete discussion of mystery and reason in Christianity can be found in the study guide titled *Living on the Ragged Edge: Coming to Terms with Reality,* ed. Bill Watkins, from the Bible-teaching ministry of Charles R. Swindoll (Fullerton, Calif.: Insight for Living, 1986), pp. 81–88.

7. See "doxa," by Sverre Aalen, in *The New International Dictionary of New Testament Theology* (Grand Rapids, Mich.: Zondervan Publishing House, 1976), vol. 2, pp. 44–48.

without canceling out or running roughshod over the free choices of human beings.

D. Majesty. God's *position* is one of eternal and almighty majesty. He is above all things—the authority over all authorities, the ruler over all rulers, the King of Kings, and the Lord of Lords (Ps. 93:1–2, Eph. 1:18–23, Col. 1:15–18, Heb. 8:1). Nothing can diminish or extinguish His greatness. However, we will never see the Father in all His splendor except through His Son. Indeed, there has never been a moment in history in which any human being has ever seen the Father directly. The Son has been the person of the Godhead who has revealed the Father to man (John 1:18, 5:37, 6:45–46; 1 Tim. 1:17, 6:16). Why the Father chose to deal with us in this way is a mystery.

IV. Some Essential Facts We Can Apply

Although some aspects of God are difficult, if not impossible, for us to fully comprehend, an accurate understanding of God should change our attitudes and behavior, not just our beliefs. With this in mind, let's zero in on some clear, practical truths that we can make a working part of our lives.

A. God is pleased when we walk by faith. "Now faith is the assurance of things hoped for, the conviction of things not seen. For by it the men of old gained approval....And without faith it is impossible to please Him, for he who comes to God must believe that He is, and that He is a rewarder of those who seek Him" (Heb. 11:1–6).

B. God is glorified when we worship in truth. " 'God is spirit, and those who worship Him must worship in spirit and truth' " (John 4:24).

C. God becomes our Father when we believe in His Son—not until.

And if Christ is in you, though the body is dead because of sin, yet the spirit is alive because of righteousness. But if the Spirit of Him who raised Jesus from the dead dwells in you, He who raised Christ Jesus from the dead will also give life to your mortal bodies through His Spirit who indwells you....For all who are being led by the Spirit of God, these are sons of God. For you have not received a spirit of slavery leading to fear again, but you have received a spirit of adoption as sons by which we cry out [to God], "Abba! Father!" (Rom. 8:10–15)

📖 Living Insights

Knowing God is life's major pursuit, yet sometimes God seems so far away. Jeremiah experienced this feeling and wrote about it in the book that bears his name. Let's look at it.

● Open your Bible to Jeremiah 29:11–14. This passage speaks of God's restoration of Judah after a seventy-year captivity. It also speaks to us of knowing God. Allow the following statements and questions to guide you as you study this passage.

—How are God's plans described in verse 11?

—What will God's plans give us?

—When we pray, what does God do?

—Verse 13 tells us how to find God. Rewrite these instructions in your own words.

—In verse 14, we see what the results of finding God can be. What are they?

📷 *Living Insights*

The main thrust of this study is the absolute importance of knowing God. We learned of five reasons for this. Using this as a page from your personal journal, write about your strengths and weaknesses, victories and struggles pertaining to each concept listed.

My Journal . . . Knowing God

1. Knowing God gives me the desire to be like Him.

_____

_____

_____

_____

_____

_____

2. Knowing God reveals the truth about myself.

_____

_____

_____

_____

_____

_____

3. Knowing God enables me to interpret my world properly.

_____

_____

_____

_____

_____

_____

Continued on next page

4. Knowing God makes me stronger and more secure.

_____

_____

_____

_____

_____

5. Knowing God introduces me to the eternal dimension of existence.

_____

_____

_____

_____

_____

_____

Loving God:
Our Ultimate Response
Deuteronomy 6:4–9, Selected Psalms

Knowing God is foundational to living a life of purpose and meaning. When we try to operate apart from Him, we end up trying to fill our emptiness with busyness, temporary highs, and cheap thrills. But nothing temporal can ever satisfy our need for the eternal. Even atheists have acknowledged this. The French atheist Albert Camus recognized that "nothing can discourage the appetite for divinity in the heart of man."[1] Walter Kaufmann even admitted that "religion is rooted in man's aspiration to transcend himself. . . . Whether he worships idols or strives to perfect himself, man is the God-intoxicated ape."[2] And Jean-Paul Sartre, another well-known atheist, let down his guard when he said, "I reached out for religion, I longed for it, it was the remedy. Had it been denied me, I would have invented it myself."[3]

However, simply having an intellectual understanding of what God is like is insufficient for experiencing the fullness of life He has to offer. We must act on our knowledge of Him by *loving* Him. And that involves trusting Him, obeying Him, and worshiping Him with our whole being. In this lesson we will explore some of what the Bible says about loving God—our ultimate response to His infinite grace and mercy.

I. A Foundational Statement and Command

Scripture's building-block passage for loving God is Deuteronomy 6:4–9. It opens with what is known in Judaism as the *Shema:* "Hear, O Israel! The Lord is our God, the Lord is one!" (v. 4). The Hebrew term used for "one" here, *echad,* is the same word used in Genesis 2:24 to describe the unity—the "one flesh" relationship—a man and a woman attain in marriage. It is also the word the men of Shechem utilized when they "[suggested] intermarriage with Jacob's children in order to become 'one people.' "[4] *Echad* "stresses unity while recognizing diversity within that oneness."[5] In Deuteronomy 6:4, Moses uses this term to convey that the Lord alone is God and that He is

1. Albert Camus, *The Rebel: An Essay on Man in Revolt* (New York, N.Y.: Alfred A. Knopf, 1956), p. 147.

2. Walter Kaufmann, *Critique of Religion and Philosophy* (New York, N.Y.: Doubleday, 1965), as quoted by Norman L. Geisler in *Is Man the Measure? An Evaluation of Contemporary Humanism* (Grand Rapids, Mich.: Baker Book House, 1983), p. 170.

3. Jean-Paul Sartre, *Words* (New York, N.Y.: George Braziller, 1964), as quoted by Geisler in *Is Man the Measure?* p. 169.

4. Herbert Wolf, " 'ehad," in *Theological Wordbook of the Old Testament,* ed. R. Laird Harris (Chicago, Ill.: Moody Press, 1980), vol. 1, p. 30.

5. Wolf, " 'ehad," p. 30.

totally unique as the one who is a plurality in oneness. Although this verse does not specify *how* God is plural yet one, it is clear in the New Testament that God's plurality is His tri-personhood as Father, Son, and Holy Spirit, and that His unity is the union of His persons in His one divine nature (Matt. 28:19, John 1:1–2, Acts 5:3–4, 2 Cor. 3:17). The statement of who God is in Deuteronomy 6:4 is followed by a command: " 'And you shall love the Lord your God with all your heart and with all your soul and with all your might' " (v. 5). Jesus said that this is the greatest commandment in the Scriptures (Matt. 22:37–38). It tells us to love God with all we are and in all we do. It calls on us to make an ultimate commitment to the ultimate being. The importance of obeying this command is emphasized in Deuteronomy 6:6–9. Here we are exhorted to love God by meditating on, teaching, and obeying His Word. Our lives should be characterized by what He desires of us. And we are to instruct our children, by our words and example, on how to mold their lives into godliness. This teaching is especially important to those of us who live in a pluralistic society—one in which many non-Christian ideologies vie for our attention and commitment. In fact, Moses instructed the people of Israel with these words when they were preparing to enter the idolatrous and affluent land of Canaan. Realizing that the Canaanites' paganism and wealth could diminish the Israelites' commitment to God, Moses exhorted them to make the Lord first in their lives. This command and the others that followed were given for the people's own welfare and survival (v. 24). Today, the Lord still wants us to place our lives under the authority of His Word. That is the way we show our love for Him (John 14:15).

II. God of Grace, God of Mercy

Our love for God is never a one-way street. Not only has He loved us first (1 John 4:7–10, 19)—He loves us infinitely more than we could ever love Him (Rom. 8:31–39). Numerous psalms express this truth. As we look at a few of them, we will see how graciously the Lord has come through for His people over and over again.

A. Psalm 31. In the opening verses of this psalm, David voices his assurance that God is the source of his strength, encouragement, guidance, and protection (vv. 1–4). He believes that the Lord will deliver him from the terrors that threaten to destroy his life (vv. 9–13). Rather than becoming intimidated and depressed, David turns to the Lord: "As for me, I trust in Thee, O Lord, / I say, 'Thou art my God.' / My times are in Thy hand; / Deliver me from the hand of my enemies, and from those who persecute me" (vv. 14–15). The Lord will never leave us high and dry. We can lean on Him no matter what, trusting in Him to see us through any trial or tribulation (compare Heb. 13:5b–6).

B. Psalm 37. This ancient hymn teaches us that God will defend us, vindicate us, and bless us. To receive this security, all we have to do is follow the counsel of the psalmist:

> Rest in the Lord and wait patiently for Him;
> Do not fret because of him who prospers in his way,
> Because of the man who carries out wicked schemes.
> Cease from anger, and forsake wrath;
> Do not fret, it leads only to evildoing.
> For evildoers will be cut off,
> But those who wait for the Lord, they will inherit the
>   land. (vv. 7–9)

Because we live in a world full of spiritual rebels, we will come under attack as we flesh out our faith. When this occurs, we need to respond to our assailants not with vengeful anger but with a caring heart (compare Rom. 12:14, 17–21). As God loves us, so should we love others (1 John 4:11).

C. Psalm 46. "God is our refuge and strength, / A very present help in trouble. / Therefore we will not fear" (vv. 1–2a). When we trust in the Lord as our greatest source of protection and power, He shows Himself to be worthy of our faith. And as He meets our needs time and time again, our fears diminish, and we grow to love Him and depend on Him more and more.

III. Man of Gratitude, Man of Love

One individual who frequently expressed his thankfulness to God was David. Much of the hymnbook we know as Psalms is comprised of his love songs to the Lord. Let's briefly consider three of David's hymns.

A. Psalm 18. The superscription of this psalm says that David wrote it "in the day that the Lord delivered him from the hand of all his enemies and from the hand of Saul." We are not told where David was. Perhaps he was hiding in a cave. Regardless of his location, he was safe—spared once again from death. Overflowing with gratitude to the Lord, David pours out his heart in lyrical form:

> "I love Thee, O Lord, my strength."
> The Lord is my rock and my fortress and my de-
>   liverer,
> My God, my rock, in whom I take refuge;
> My shield and the horn of my salvation, my strong-
>   hold.
> I call upon the Lord, who is worthy to be praised,
> And I am saved from my enemies.
> (vv. 1–3)

The Lord lives, and blessed be my rock;
And exalted be the God of my salvation,
The God who executes vengeance for me,
And subdues peoples under me.…
Therefore I will give thanks to Thee among the
    nations, O Lord,
And I will sing praises to Thy name.
(vv. 46–49)

David's love for God is manifest in the praise and thanksgiving he offered.

B. Psalm 32. This song was composed against a very different backdrop. David had not been fleeing for his life but lying to the Hebrew people. He had slept with another man's wife and had her husband killed so that he could take her as his bride. After his sin was finally exposed by a prophet of God, David readily confessed his wrongdoing and experienced the Lord's discipline and forgiveness (2 Sam. 11:1–12:25, Ps. 51). In response to God's gracious dealing with him, David penned these words:

How blessed is he whose transgression is forgiven,
Whose sin is covered!
How blessed is the man to whom the Lord does not
    impute iniquity,
And in whose spirit there is no deceit!
When I kept silent about my sin, my body wasted away
Through my groaning all day long.
For day and night Thy hand was heavy upon me;
My vitality was drained away as with the fever heat
    of summer.
I acknowledged my sin to Thee,
And my iniquity I did not hide;
I said, "I will confess my transgressions to the Lord";
And *Thou didst forgive the guilt of my sin.*
(Ps. 32:1–5, emphasis added)

The Lord dealt not only with David's sin but also with the guilt he had experienced as a result of his sin. Consequently, David no longer felt the pangs of guilt—only the joy of divine cleansing and restoration.

C. Psalm 40. Although we are not told exactly what occasioned the writing of this song, we do know that David composed it after the Lord had delivered him from a long period of struggle (vv. 1–2a). God, in His mercy, rescued David and strengthened him once again in his faith. Notice how David expresses his gratitude to the Lord:

He brought me up out of the pit of destruction, out
    of the miry clay;

And He set my feet upon a rock making my footsteps
firm.
And He put a new song in my mouth, a song of praise
to our God;
Many will see and fear,
And will trust in the Lord.
How blessed is the man who has made the Lord his
trust. (vv. 2–4a)

IV. For Those Who Truly Love God

David's responses to God's grace provide a worthy model for us to
imitate. Indeed, David shows us that those who really love the Lord
are those who have properly responded to His love for them. Reflecting on David's psalms, we can make at least three observations
about those of us who have a genuine love for God.

**A. We who truly love God have experienced His power
to deliver, so our fears are gone.**

**B. We who truly love God have received His peace and
forgiveness, so our guilt has been relieved.**

**C. We who truly love God have felt His presence through
affliction and, as a result, our faith has been strengthened.**

Continued on next page

Study One ▬▬▬▬▬▬▬▬▬▬▬▬▬▬▬▬▬▬▬▬▬▬▬▬▬

Where can you turn in the Scriptures for words of praise, worship, and thanksgiving, as well as other appropriate responses to God? That's correct—the Psalms! Let's look at how the writers of these hymns describe our God and how we should respond to Him.

● The following chart lists the psalms we briefly observed in our study. Read them now in greater detail, jotting down the words and phrases that speak of God's greatness and what our response should be.

Loving God: Our Ultimate Response	
Descriptions of God	Appropriate Responses
Psalm 18	
Psalm 31	

Descriptions of God	Appropriate Responses
Psalm 32	
Psalm 37	

Continued on next page

Descriptions of God	Appropriate Responses
Psalm 40	
Psalm 46	

Living Insights

In study one we looked at several psalms. Their majestic words are actually lyrics to songs that were sung as part of the temple worship.

● Let's look at some modern songs of praise to God. Locate a hymn-book (perhaps your church will allow you to borrow one) and page through the hymns. Under the headings below, list some hymns that speak of *knowing* God and some that talk of *loving* God. Don't limit your lists to songs you know; broaden your horizons by learning hymns that are new to you. If you're in a group, sing together some of the favorites you discover. If you're studying alone, sing by yourself to the Lord or just meditate on the richness found in the music of His people.

Praise Hymns

Knowing God	Loving God
_____	_____
_____	_____
_____	_____
_____	_____
_____	_____
_____	_____
_____	_____
_____	_____
_____	_____
_____	_____
_____	_____
_____	_____
_____	_____
_____	_____

Mary's Little Lamb
Luke 2, Micah 5, Isaiah 7

In 1809, the eyes of the world were riveted on Napoleon—the general who was pushing his way through Europe in a mad pursuit of power. No one seemed to know that the really significant events were occurring outside of the limelight, in private homes. While Napoleon was conquering Europe, William Gladstone was born, who later became one of England's finest statesmen. In the same year Alfred Tennyson took his first breaths of life. His literary endeavors eventually left their mark on his world and the generations that followed. Charles Darwin, author of *The Origin of Species* and popularizer of biological evolution, also began his days on earth in 1809. And a man who altered the course of American history was born in a rugged log cabin that same year. His name? Abraham Lincoln. But as significant as these births were, none can compare to the birth of a baby boy that took place in 5 or 4 B.C.[1] At that time, the seat of world power was Rome, and most of Europe, northern Africa, and the Middle Eastern countries were under its dominion. Hardly anyone cared about the small town of Bethlehem, much less the birth of a Jewish infant named Jesus—the one who would die on a cross for the sins of all mankind. God, however, saw things differently. He moved a physician named Luke to record in his Gospel the basic facts about Jesus. Let's turn our eyes to what Luke tells us about the most significant birth in human history.

I. The Backdrop for Jesus' Birth

Luke links the birth of Jesus with a decree given by Caesar Augustus, the highest-ranked governing official in the Roman Empire. Augustus demanded that a census be taken of all those who lived under Roman rule (Luke 2:1). Since the Roman Empire stretched from the Atlantic Ocean to the Euphrates, from the Danube and Rhine to the Sahara Desert, this would have been a tremendous task. But it needed to be done for taxation purposes. Censuses were taken periodically, so Luke identifies the one he is referring to as "the first census taken while Quirinius was governor of Syria" (v. 2).

A. The time of the census. According to New Testament scholar Harold Hoehner, the census mentioned by Luke "was probably taken sometime between 6 and 4 B.C., preferably the latter part of this span of time. This fits well with both Matthew's and Luke's chronologies [of Jesus], which seem to indicate that the census and Christ's birth were shortly before Herod's death."[2]

---

1. The justification for adopting this date is given in Harold W. Hoehner's *Chronological Aspects of the Life of Christ* (Grand Rapids, Mich.: Zondervan Publishing House, 1977), chap. 1.

2. Hoehner, *Chronological Aspects*, p. 23.

B. The political situation. Herod the Great "was proclaimed king of the Jews by the Roman Senate in late 40 B.C."[3] However, he did not take control of Palestine until "the summer of 37 B.C. when, with the help of the Roman army, Jerusalem was captured and Antigonus removed [as ruler of the Jews]."[4] Always maintaining his loyalty to Rome, Herod reigned over the Jews for thirty-four years. Just days prior to his death in the spring of 4 B.C., he composed a will requesting that his domain be divided among his three sons—Archelaus, Philip, and Antipas. For the most part, Caesar Augustus honored Herod's final request. The domain was apportioned, with Judea and Samaria being given to Archelaus to rule. This decision proved to be a mistake. Archelaus reigned with an iron fist, motivated by bigotry. His cruelty brought two communities together that were usually bitter enemies—the Jews and the Samaritans. They brought a formal complaint against Archelaus, which, in part, led to his removal from office in A.D. 6. Several years earlier (around 6 B.C.), when Herod the Great was still ruling over the Jews, Augustus assigned Publius Quirinius the task of taking a census—"a process which always enraged the . . . Jews."[5]

C. The impact on Jesus' birth. Centuries before Palestine became a Roman province, the Lord declared that a divinely appointed ruler for Israel would be born in Bethlehem (Micah 5:2). This king's " 'goings forth,' " announced God, " 'are from long ago,/ From the days of eternity' " (v. 2b). How incredible it must have seemed that a mighty, divine ruler would be born in a small, insignificant town like Bethlehem! And yet, one of the requirements of Augustus's census was that all the people had to return to their hometowns to register (Luke 2:3). This demand set a Jewish couple on a strenuous eighty-mile trek from Nazareth to Bethlehem. The young woman, Mary, was pregnant and engaged to be married. Her fiancé, Joseph, perhaps using the census as an excuse to "[remove] Mary from possible gossip and emotional stress in her own village,"[6] took her to his hometown (vv. 4–5). In comparison to all that was happening in Palestine at the time, this couple's experience must have seemed

---

3. Harold W. Hoehner, *Herod Antipas* (Grand Rapids, Mich.: Zondervan Publishing House, 1972), p. 6.

4. Hoehner, *Herod Antipas,* p. 7.

5. E. M. Blaiklock, "Quirinius," in *The Zondervan Pictorial Encyclopedia of the Bible* (Grand Rapids, Mich.: Regency Reference Library, Zondervan Publishing House, 1976), vol. 5, p. 6.

6. Walter L. Liefeld, "Luke," in *The Expositor's Bible Commentary* (Grand Rapids, Mich.: Regency Reference Library, Zondervan Publishing House, 1984), vol. 8, p. 844.

trivial to most people. But in God's plan, Mary's pregnancy and Joseph's decision to take her with him to Bethlehem were setting the stage of human history for the birth of man's Savior—Jesus the Christ.

II. The Scene in Bethlehem
When Mary and Joseph arrived in Bethlehem, they encountered a town bursting at the seams with people who had come to register for the census. The young couple looked in vain for a place to stay. All the usual lodging places were occupied (v. 7b). Desperate to find shelter, they settled in a place used to house animals. Tradition has it that this place was actually a cave that had been turned into a stable.[7] It was there that Mary writhed in pain until "she gave birth to her first-born son" (v. 7a). To keep Him warm, protect His limbs from harm, and give Him a sense of security, Mary wrapped her newborn baby in long strips of cloth and placed Him in a feeding trough filled with hay (v. 7b).

III. Mary's Lamb
As Joseph and Mary looked at their baby boy, they may have reflected on these words from Isaiah: " 'The Lord Himself will give you a sign: Behold, a virgin will be with child and bear a son, and she will call His name Immanuel' " (Isa. 7:14). Joseph knew that he was only the legal father of the child, not His biological father. And Joseph had learned from angelic pronouncement that Mary's pregnancy was not due to any man but to the Holy Spirit, who had caused her to conceive by some unrevealed, miraculous means (Matt. 1:18–25; compare Luke 1:26–38). Now, here in a manger lay the Son of God in human flesh, born to a virgin. Mary and Joseph must have sat in awe! Nearby, some shepherds were "staying out in the fields, and keeping watch over their flock by night" (Luke 2:8). Some Bible scholars suggest that these sheep were being raised to be sacrificed at Passover.[8] In the coldness of this dark night, the shepherds received an unexpected visit from an angel. This messenger was accompanied by the almost blinding light of the glory of the Lord. The shepherds shrank back in fear (v. 9), but the angel spoke words of comfort, announcing what Jews had been longing to hear for centuries: " 'Do not be afraid; for behold, I bring you good news of a great joy which shall be for all the people; for today in the city of David there has been born for you a Savior, who is Christ the Lord. And this will be a sign to you: you will find a baby wrapped in cloths, and lying in a manger' " (vv. 10–12).

7. See F. F. Bruce, *Jesus and Paul: Places They Knew* (Nashville, Tenn.: Thomas Nelson Publishers, 1981), p. 8.

8. See Liefeld, "Luke," p. 845.

IV. The Significance of the Insignificant

Things today are much the same as they were in the days of Mary and Joseph. Few people seem to know or care about what God is doing in the world. Even at Christmas, the traditional celebration of Christ's birth, one hardly hears mention of Jesus or the reason He came to Earth. Instead, the focus of people's lives is still on the insignificant, the temporal, the perishable. Is that where *your* eyes are fixed? Are you crowding Jesus out of your life with the clutter of all that is so much less important? There is not a more life-changing, beneficial thing you can do than to make Christ the foundation and center of your life. If you have never trusted in Him as your Savior, do so now. Let Him come into your heart and give you a new life filled with God's imperishable riches. If you have already made Mary's Lamb your personal Savior, continue to give Him complete authority over your life. Put Him first in everything by daily submitting every aspect of your life to Him and His Word.

Living Insights

Study One ▰▰▰▰▰▰▰▰▰▰▰▰▰▰▰▰▰▰▰▰▰▰▰▰▰▰▰▰▰▰

The Christmas story is such a well-known story—but we seem to isolate its use to the month of December. If it is December as you read this, fine; but if it's not, that's even better. Let's do some Christmas celebrating!

- The account of Christ's birth in Luke 2 is familiar to most of us, but have you ever tried to recount it in your own words? This method of Bible study is called *paraphrasing*. Write out Luke 2 in words of your own choosing. Try to bring out the meanings and emotions woven between the lines of this great chapter. Merry Christmas!

My Paraphrase of Luke 2

_____

_____

_____

_____

_____

_____

Continued on next page

My Paraphrase of Luke 2—Continued

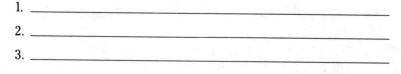

Living Insights

Have you ever asked Christ Jesus to occupy your heart as He once occupied the manger? That is, have you received Him as your personal Savior? Let's consider this all-important decision.

- If you have never received Christ into your life, do it now in the quietness of your own mind. Talk to God honestly. If you're searching for words, say something like this: "Dear Lord Jesus, I know I can't do anything to save myself, but You died on the cross to deliver me from my sins. So right now I accept You as my personal Savior. I believe You died and rose again for me." If you say words like these to the Lord, believing the message they convey, you'll become a child of God . . . a servant of the King! Don't delay.
- If you already know Christ as your Redeemer, jot down the names of two or three friends who have not trusted in Him. Begin praying for them by name. Perhaps God will give *you* the opportunity to present Christ to them.

Friends I Want to Pray For

1. _____

2. _____

3. _____

When the God-Man
Walked among Us

Selections from the Gospels

All the world's major religions are dominated by a great leader or teacher. In Buddhism the central figure is Siddharta Gautama, known as the Buddha. The founder of Islam is Muhammed, and the most significant prophet of Judaism is Moses. As revered as these men are, none of them are indispensable to their respective religions. The main teachings of their faiths can stand alone—apart from the personalities that were instrumental in their birth. Christianity, on the other hand, is altogether different. As John Stott explains:

> Essentially Christianity is Christ. The person and work of Christ are the rock upon which the Christian religion is built. If he is not who he said he was, and if he did not do what he said he had come to do, the foundation is undermined and the whole superstructure will collapse. Take Christ from Christianity, and you disembowel it; there is practically nothing left. Christ is the centre of Christianity; all else is circumference.[1]

Who is this one who is so special, so indispensable? Let's turn to the Bible and find out.

I. Who Is Jesus Christ?

The pages of history are replete with various answers to this question. He has been thought of as a mere man, a persuasive demon, one of many gods, and as God Himself in human form. Concepts of Him in His own day were just as varied. The Gospels record many of these ideas as well as Christ's thoughts about His own identity. Let's look at these historical records in our search to discover who Jesus really is.

A. The wise men.
"Now after Jesus was born in Bethlehem . . . , behold, magi from the east arrived in Jerusalem, saying, 'Where is He who has been born King of the Jews? For we saw His star in the east, and have come to worship Him'" (Matt. 2:1–2). Exactly who the magi were is uncertain. We do know that in New Testament times, the term *magi* "loosely covered a wide variety of men interested in dreams, astrology, magic, books thought to contain mysterious references to the future, and the like. Some Magi honestly inquired after truth; many were rogues and charlatans"[2]

1. John R. W. Stott, *Basic Christianity* (Downers Grove, Ill.: InterVarsity Press, 1958), p. 21.

2. D. A. Carson, "Matthew," in *The Expositor's Bible Commentary* (Grand Rapids, Mich.: Regency Reference Library, Zondervan Publishing House, 1984), vol. 8, p. 85.

(see Acts 8:9, 13:6–11). The magi who sought the infant Jesus believed that He was the king of the Jews. There was no doubt in their minds that this newborn child was a monarch who deserved their homage and gifts (Matt. 2:2, 11).

B. God the Father. When Jesus was about thirty years of age, He went to the Jordan River to be baptized by John the Baptist (Matt. 3:13, Luke 3:21–23). As Christ came out of the water, "a voice out of the heavens [said], 'This is My beloved Son, in whom I am well-pleased'" (Matt. 3:17). God the Father, the one who cannot lie (Titus 1:2), acknowledged that Jesus was His Son and of the same divine essence as Himself.

C. The Pharisees. At the opposite end of the spectrum from God the Father were the Pharisees. Although these religious leaders frequently referred to Jesus as "teacher" or "rabbi" (Matt. 9:11, John 3:1–2), they also accused Him of being empowered by demons (Matt. 9:34, 12:24). Christ steadfastly rejected this charge as ridiculous, pointing out that if Satan had given Him the power to cast out demons, he would have been defeating himself and thereby destroying his own kingdom (12:25–26).

D. John the Baptizer. When John first saw Jesus, he recognized that Christ was the Son of God, the long-awaited Messiah (John 1:29, 34). However, during Jesus' ministry in Galilee, John was imprisoned, perhaps for as long as a year. While confined, John began to have second thoughts about Jesus' identity. After all, John had proclaimed a Savior who would bless those who believed and judge those who would not (Matt. 3:11–12). Instead, Jesus was preaching repentance and forgiveness; He was healing many but apparently judging none. So "when John . . . heard of the works of Christ, he sent word by his disciples, and said to Him, 'Are you the Expected One, or shall we look for someone else?'" (11:2–3). John's doubts got the better of him. He was no longer sure about who Christ was.

E. Jesus' neighbors and immediate family. More questions about Jesus' identity came from those who watched Him grow up. On a visit to His hometown, Nazareth, the people asked, "'Where did this man get this wisdom, and these miraculous powers? Is not this the carpenter's son? Is not His mother called Mary, and His brothers, James and Joseph and Simon and Judas? And His sisters, are they not all with us? Where then did this man get all these things?'" (13:54b–56). In one sense, their questions are understandable. How did an ordinary man with no special education gain such extraordinary wisdom and power? On the other hand, their queries reveal that they were not seeking answers but expressing their rejection of Jesus as the Messiah.

In their minds, He was only the son of a carpenter, not the Son of God. Adding sorrow to heartache, members of Christ's own family refused to believe in His claims (John 7:5). On one occasion, they even tried to seize Him and remove Him from public ministry on the grounds that He had " 'lost His senses' " (Mark 3:21).

F. Herod the Tetrarch. Herod Antipas, the son of Herod the Great, began ruling over Galilee and Peraea about a year after his father's death. When he learned of Jesus' teaching and miracles, he feared that Christ was actually John the Baptist, risen from the dead to haunt and judge him (Matt. 14:1–2). Herod must have felt guilty about his execution of John. He had been tricked into beheading the prophet by his brother's wife, who was angry with John for his denunciation of her immoral relationship with Herod (vv. 3–11).

G. The general public. On one occasion, Jesus asked His disciples who people thought He was (16:13). "And they said, 'Some say John the Baptist; and others, Elijah; but still others, Jeremiah, or one of the prophets' " (v. 14). The general public obviously had a high view of Christ, thinking He was one of the great prophets. However, it is also evident that few grasped the fact that Jesus was the Son of God, Savior of all mankind.

H. Peter, the disciple. During the same conversation, Christ asked His disciples who they thought He was (v. 15). Peter responded correctly: " 'Thou art the Christ, the Son of the living God' " (v. 16).

I. The citizens of Jerusalem. Toward the end of Jesus' ministry, He entered Jerusalem on the back of a donkey, thus fulfilling prophecy (21:1–7). As He entered the city, people surrounded Him, "crying out . . . saying, 'Hosanna to the Son of David; / Blessed is He who comes in the name of the Lord; / Hosanna in the highest!' " (v. 9). Some of the inhabitants of Jerusalem recognized Jesus as the Messiah who was to come through David's line, although many of them were still unsure (v. 10).

J. Caiaphas, the high priest. After Christ was betrayed by Judas Iscariot (26:47–50), He was placed on trial. Among those He was brought before was Caiaphas, high priest of the Jews and head of the religious body known as the Sanhedrin. Caiaphas interrogated Jesus about His identity, asking Him if He was " 'the Christ, the Son of God' " (v. 63). Jesus acknowledged that He was the Messiah and that one day He would reign with God and return as the judge of mankind (v. 64). Caiaphas could listen to no more. In a fit of rage, he tore his robes and charged Christ with blasphemy (v. 65). Then he and the Sanhedrin dedicated themselves to getting Jesus put to death (v. 66, 27:1–2).

K. Pilate. Since Jews did not have the civil authority to carry out capital punishment, the Sanhedrin led Jesus before Pontius Pilate, the Roman governor of Judea. Pilate asked Him if He was the king of the Jews (27:11a). Christ said that He was (v. 11b; compare John 18:28–37). After further questioning, Pilate concluded that Jesus had done nothing to warrant civil punishment (John 18:38b). But the people, intent on having Christ executed (19:4–15), pressured Pilate into ordering Jesus' crucifixion (v. 16). The charge against Him was painted on a sign that was nailed to His cross: " 'Jesus the Nazarene, the King of the Jews' " (v. 19). The chief priests tried to get Pilate to change the wording of the sign, but he would not (vv. 21–22).

L. Jesus Himself. After Jesus was officially proclaimed dead (Mark 15:42–45), He was quickly buried (John 19:31–42). Three days later, His tomb was discovered empty, and He was seen—alive (John 20:1–18)! Sometime later, Christ demonstrated to the eleven disciples that He had physically risen from the grave (Luke 24:36–43; compare Acts 1:1–3). Then He turned their focus toward the Old Testament, helping them to realize that He was the Messiah spoken about in the Scriptures (Luke 24:44–47). Jesus believed Himself to be the Son of God . . . deity clothed in human flesh . . . the Savior of the world. And He verified His claims by fulfilling prophecy, living a sinless life, teaching with supernatural authority, performing miracles, and rising from the dead. No wonder John, toward the end of his account of Christ's earthly ministry, penned these words: "Many other signs therefore Jesus also performed in the presence of the disciples, which are not written in this book; but these have been written that you may believe that Jesus is the Christ, the Son of God; and that believing you may have life in His name" (John 20:30–31).

II. Some Examples of Christ's Humanity and Deity

We have seen that Jesus was both fully God and fully man. The Gospels contain many illustrations of this fact. Let's probe further into one example per Gospel.

A. Matthew 14:22–33. In this passage we see Jesus climbing up a mountainside alone to pray (vv. 22–23). The fact that He brings petitions before God the Father shows that He is human, since deity is without need (Acts 17:24–25). Man, on the other hand, cannot even breathe without God's sustaining power (vv. 25b; compare John 15:5, Col. 1:17). During Jesus' time in prayer, the disciples get trapped in a severe storm while sailing across the lake (Matt. 14:24). Christ responds by walking toward them across the water (v. 25). After joining them in the boat,

He stops the storm (vv. 27–32). Christ's exercise of authority over nature prompts the disciples to worship Him, acknowledging His deity (v. 33).

B. Mark 1:40–42. In this scene a man approaches Jesus, begging Him to cleanse him of leprosy. The man's choice of words, "Make me clean," is important. In the Old Testament, leprosy is an illustration of sin. Anyone who had the dreaded disease was ostracized from the Jewish community (Lev. 13:45–46). But this man violates the Mosaic Law by approaching Christ, beseeching Him to heal him. Looking down on the leper kneeling before Him, Jesus perhaps sees bleeding stumps where fingers once were, or maybe His eyes fall on a tear-stained, disfigured face. He certainly sees a man deeply hurt by years of rejection. Jesus knows that He can legally turn away from this man and go His own way. Instead, moved within His humanity to act mercifully, Jesus reaches out and touches the untouchable, speaking the words the leper longed to hear: " 'I am willing; be cleansed' " (v. 41b). Suddenly, the disease is gone and, for all we know, lost limbs unexpectedly grow back and scarred physical features become like new (v. 42). The man is healed in body and soul; he stands forgiven and restored. Only God could have performed such a wonder.

C. Luke 8:22–25. On another occasion, we see Jesus getting into a boat with His disciples and telling them to sail to the other side of the lake (v. 22). Christ falls asleep during their trip (v. 23a), revealing His humanity once again (compare Ps. 121:2–4). Soon, the water splashing against the side of the boat in peaceful rhythm becomes life-endangering waves that thrash and threaten to flood the vessel (Luke 8:23b). The disciples panic and wake their Master (v. 24a). Jesus tells the storm to stop—and it does (v. 24b). Calm returns to the lake, but not to the disciples. With feelings of respect, terror, and awe, they ask one another, " 'Who then is this, that He commands even the winds and the water, and they obey Him?' " (v. 25). The disciples were right to ask this question. They had seen a man do something only deity can do.

D. John 11:1–44. In this story, Jesus receives word that Lazarus, His close friend, is sick. He delays going to him for two days (vv. 1–7), lingering long enough for Lazarus to die (vv. 11–15). Arriving at the outskirts of Bethany, Jesus is greeted by both of Lazarus's sisters, who blame Him for their brother's death (vv. 20–21, 30–32). The sight of the grief-stricken women and the Jews who are mourning with them stirs Christ's human emotions (v. 33). After being led to the tomb of Lazarus, Jesus' feelings spill forth in weeping, again revealing His humanity (vv. 34–35). Pulling Himself together, Jesus commands the mourners to remove the stone covering the entrance to the tomb (vv. 39b–41a). Jesus pauses, raises His eyes heavenward, and thanks His Father for hearing His prayer (vv. 41b–42). Then, with the authority of deity, He shouts, " 'Lazarus, come forth!' " (v. 43). The impossible happens. The friend who had been dead for four days appears at the mouth of his tomb, wrapped in funeral garb . . . but alive (v. 44)! The Son of God had spoken.

III. The Verdict of History

No individual in human history has raised more controversy concerning His identity than Jesus. Though many have believed Him to be who He said He was, others have viewed Him as nothing more than a man, a wise moral teacher. C. S. Lewis has pointed out the fallacy in this kind of thinking:

> People often say about Him: "I'm ready to accept Jesus as a great moral teacher, but I don't accept His claim to be God." That is the one thing we must not say. A man who was merely a man and said the sort of things Jesus said would not be a great moral teacher. He would either be a lunatic—on a level with a man who says he is a poached egg—or else he would be the Devil of Hell. You must make your choice. Either this man was, and is, the Son of God: or else a madman or something worse. You can shut Him up for a fool, you can spit at Him and kill Him as a demon; or you can fall at His feet and call Him Lord and God. But let us not come with any patronising nonsense about His being a great human teacher. He has not left that open to us. He did not intend to.[3]

Who do *you* believe Christ is? The verdict of history is clear: He is the God-man, the Lord and Redeemer of the world.

Living Insights

Study One

In the lesson, we observed a different example of Christ's humanity and deity from each of the four Gospels. Now let's examine one event that is recorded in all four Gospels—Jesus' feeding of more than five thousand people.

- Read the passages listed in the following chart. Look for similarities between the accounts, and then look for peculiarities—tidbits about the story recorded in only one of the Gospels.

Continued on next page

3. C. S. Lewis, *Mere Christianity* (New York, N.Y.: Macmillan Publishing Co., 1952), p. 56.

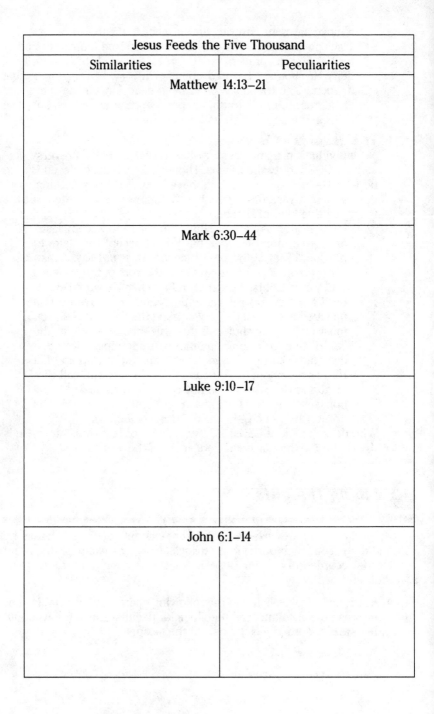

Jesus Feeds the Five Thousand	
Similarities	Peculiarities
Matthew 14:13–21	
Mark 6:30–44	
Luke 9:10–17	
John 6:1–14	

Living Insights

The accounts of incidents in Christ's earthly life are usually favorite portions of the Bible. Here's an opportunity for you to reflect on them.

- What is your favorite story about Jesus? Why?

_____

_____

_____

_____

_____

- What is your favorite attribute of Christ's character? Why?

_____

_____

_____

_____

_____

- What is your favorite miracle of Christ's? Why?

_____

_____

_____

_____

_____

Continued on next page

67

- What is your favorite description of Jesus? Why?

_____

_____

_____

_____

_____

- Which writer do you think best describes Christ—Matthew, Mark, Luke, or John? Why?

_____

_____

_____

_____

_____

- If you could go back in time in order to personally witness one event in Jesus' life, which event would it be? Why?

_____

_____

_____

_____

_____

Changing Lives Is Jesus' Business

John 4, 9, 20

Becoming an adult...moving from one city to another...receiving a promotion...going off to college. These experiences have something in common. They all involve change. Indeed, change permeates every facet of our lives. Sometimes we welcome change; other times we do not. But regardless of our outlook, two things are certain: the key to changing the world is changing people, and the key to changing people is bringing them into a right relationship with Christ. We can alter structures, environments, or governments—but unless hearts are softened toward the Savior, people's lives will not be different. Let's explore this truth.

I. God's Commitment to Changing Lives

God's specialty is changing people. Because He wants us to grow in godliness, He takes an active role in helping us toward this goal. Let's briefly examine some biblical texts that reveal His personal involvement.

A. Jeremiah 18:1–6. During Jeremiah's ministry, the Lord commanded him to visit a potter's house (vv. 1–2). There he saw a potter molding a lump of clay into a useful pot (v. 3). When a flaw appeared in the vessel, the potter pressed and prodded the clay, reshaping it until the clay became a vessel with which he was pleased (v. 4). "Then the word of the Lord came to [Jeremiah] saying, 'Can I not, O house of Israel, deal with you as this potter does?...Behold, like the clay in the potter's hand, so are you in My hand, O house of Israel' " (v. 6). The Hebrews were the object of God's care. They belonged to the Lord; consequently, He promised to continue shaping them into the kind of people He desired them to be—even if that required the firm hand of divine discipline (compare vv. 7–11).

B. Isaiah 64:8. In this passage, God is again recognized as the shaper of His people: "Now, O Lord, Thou art our Father, / We are the clay, and Thou our potter; / And all of us are the work of Thy hand."

C. 1 Samuel 10:6–9. A flesh-and-blood example of God's molding ministry is Saul. After he was annointed as the first king of Israel, the Holy Spirit dramatically changed Saul's character and enabled him to prophesy—all in one day! Although the Lord does not always change us as rapidly and easily as He did Saul, He is committed to our development, regardless of the time or pain it may require.

D. Proverbs 21:1. No human being—not a stubborn husband, an accomplished athlete, a strong-willed child, a high-ranking military commander, or even an influential government official—

can escape the Potter's hands. As Proverbs 21:1 states, "The king's heart [and everyone else's] is like channels of water in the hand of the Lord; He turns it wherever He wishes."

E. Romans 8:28–30. In this text, the Apostle Paul reminds us that "God causes all things to work together for good to those who love [Him]" (v. 28). The "good" that God has in mind is the conforming of believers into "the image of His Son" (v. 29). God the Father wants His people to have the character of Christ, and He will not stop working toward this objective until it is accomplished in the life of every Christian (v. 30; compare Jude 24).

F. Ephesians 2:10. God is so involved in the lives of believers that He refers to them as "His workmanship." They are *His* project, "created in Christ Jesus for good works, which God prepared beforehand."

G. Philippians 1:6. This passage assures us that what God starts, He finishes. He will not walk away from anyone. He will woo us, pursue us, purge us, refine us, and polish us until He perfects us in "the day of Christ Jesus." Now that's encouraging!

II. Three Lives Jesus Changed

Let's move from general statements to specific examples. In the Gospel of John, we discover three people whose lives were greatly altered by the Son of God. Although these individuals differed from one another in significant ways, all three were like clay in the hands of the divine Potter.

A. A wayward woman. During the heat of the day, a Samaritan woman came to draw water at the local well (John 4:7a). Sitting by the well was Jesus, resting from His journey and waiting for His disciples to return with some food (vv. 6, 8). Jesus asked the woman to give Him a drink (v. 7b). She was surprised (v. 9) because she knew that Jews believed that "Samaritan women were . . . continually menstruating and thus unclean. Therefore a Jew who drank from a Samaritan woman's vessel would become ceremonially unclean."[1] Jesus responded to this woman by telling her that He could give her " 'living water' " (v. 10). She completely missed Jesus' point, thinking He was talking about fresh spring water rather than everlasting spiritual water (vv. 11–12). Even when Jesus clarified what He had meant, she still failed to understand (vv. 13–15). So Christ changed His strategy and addressed her most basic problem. He asked her to get her husband (v. 16). She replied that she had no husband. Jesus commended

---

1. Edwin A. Blum, "John," in *The Bible Knowledge Commentary: New Testament Edition,* ed. John F. Walvoord and Roy B. Zuck (Wheaton, Ill.: Victor Books, 1983), p. 285. See also "The Gospel of John," by Merrill C. Tenney, in *The Expositor's Bible Commentary* (Grand Rapids, Mich.: Regency Reference Library, Zondervan Publishing House, 1981), vol. 9, pp. 54–55.

her honesty, revealed His knowledge of her marital past, and exposed her immorality (vv. 17–18). His answer raised Him to the status of a prophet in the woman's sight (v. 19), yet she still showed no sign of wanting to repent. In fact, she tried to side-track Jesus by raising an ancient religious issue that was still a matter of friction between Jews and Samaritans (v. 20). But Christ used this dispute as a vehicle to declare His messiahship (vv. 21–26). At this juncture, the disciples returned and "marveled that He had been speaking with a woman" (v. 27). The Samaritan woman seized the opportunity to leave Jesus and spread word about Him in the city (vv. 28–29). Her testimony brought the city's inhabitants out to meet Christ (v. 30). The result? Not only was the woman saved, but many other Samaritans placed their faith in Christ as well (vv. 39–42). Jesus changed her life and the lives of many people through her witness.

B. A blind beggar. On another occasion, Jesus and His disciples came across a beggar who had been blind from birth (9:1). Rather than reaching out to this man with compassion, the disciples used his plight to raise a theological question (v. 2). Perhaps they had grown callous toward beggars because they were such a common sight in Palestine. Jesus answered the disciples' query (vv. 3–5) and proceeded to restore the blind man's sight (vv. 6–7). This healing created quite a sensation. Many of the beggar's neighbors and acquaintances couldn't believe that he was the same man (vv. 8–9). When the beggar reassured them of his identity and explained how Jesus had healed him, they took him to the Pharisees (vv. 10–13). The beggar's testimony before these religious leaders sparked a controversy among them concerning who Jesus was (v. 16). However, regardless of what the beggar said, the Pharisees refused to believe that he had ever been blind (vv. 17–18a). In an attempt to settle the issue, these religious authorities summoned the man's parents (vv. 18–19). They identified the beggar as their son and confirmed that he had been born blind (v. 20)—but, afraid of being excommunicated from the synagogue, they would not support their son's story of healing (vv. 21–23). Their cowardice, however, did not thwart their son's persistence. In fact, the beggar argued with the Pharisees, contending that his miraculous healing was ample evidence that Jesus came from God (vv. 24–33). Sometime after the beggar's excommunication, he was approached by Jesus (vv. 34–35a). Christ explained to him who He was, and the beggar trusted in Him for his salvation (vv. 35b–38). The man walked away restored, not only in body but also in soul.

C. A doubting disciple. During Jesus' earthly ministry, the disciple Thomas had shown his commitment to Christ by expressing his willingness to die with Him (11:16). Now, however, Jesus was dead ... and Thomas was greatly disillusioned and grief-stricken. When Thomas heard the other disciples report seeing Jesus alive again, he would not believe them. He said that personally seeing the crucified Christ alive would be the only way to resolve his deep-seated doubt (20:25). Several days later, Christ reappeared to the disciples, and this time Thomas was with them (v. 26). Jesus produced the evidence Thomas had needed, and this doubting disciple responded by expressing faith in Christ as his Lord and God (vv. 27–29). Once more, Jesus broke down the walls that separated Him from someone who needed Him—and once again, He changed a life for eternity.

III. What about You?

The same Lord who changed an immoral Samaritan woman, a blind beggar, and a skeptical disciple is committed to changing you. He will not give up on you. However, you can either cooperate with Him or resist His work in your life. If you are fighting Him, will you yield and submit to Him today? He desires to give you only the best (Matt. 7:7–11; Rom. 8:28, 32). So relax, and let Him have His way.

Living Insights

Study One

A wayward woman, a blind beggar, and a doubting disciple are three examples of people whose lives were changed by Christ while He was on earth. Let's look at three stories from the book of Acts that describe lives He changed even after He ascended into heaven.

- Look up the three references listed in the following chart. As you read, notice how the people were described before they met Christ. Then contrast that with how they were described after they received Jesus. Some accounts have greater detail than others, but each one is illuminating in its own way.

Changing Lives Is Jesus' Business	
Acts 2:1–47 Those at Pentecost	
Before Meeting Christ	After Receiving Christ
Acts 9:1–22 Paul on the Damascus Road	
Before Meeting Christ	After Receiving Christ

Continued on next page

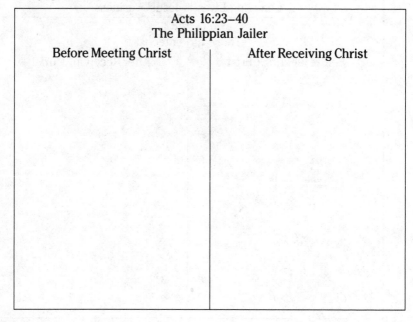

Acts 16:23–40 The Philippian Jailer	
Before Meeting Christ	After Receiving Christ

 Living Insights

Study Two

We've seen how Jesus changed the woman at the well, the blind beggar, the doubting disciple, Saul of Tarsus, the Philippian jailer, and thousands at the day of Pentecost. The question of utmost importance at this point is: How has Jesus changed *your* life?

● Using this as a page from your journal, write about Christ's impact in your life.

How Jesus Changed My Life

1. My Life before Christ _____

_____

_____

_____

_____

_____

_____

_____

_____

_____

_____

2. How I Met the Lord _____

_____

_____

_____

_____

_____

_____

_____

_____

3. Changes in My Life since I Received Jesus _____

_____

_____

_____

_____

_____

_____

_____

_____

_____

The Spirit Who Is Not a Ghost
John 16:1–15

Something that we can't see, smell, touch, or taste helps keep us alive. It can also cool down a hot day, dry out a flooded field, overturn a ship, and topple a building. When properly controlled in a network of hoses and valves, it can bring a commercial bus, an eighteen-wheeler, or a hundred-car train to a screeching halt. What is this mysterious force? Air. It may surprise you that the Bible uses the words for *air* in reference to the Third Person of the Trinity—the Holy Spirit (Ezek. 37:1–14, John 3:5–8). In the Old Testament the word for *wind* or *breath* is *ruach,* and in the New Testament it is *pnuema.* According to J. I. Packer, "the picture [given by these words] is of air made to move vigorously, even violently, and the thought that the picture expresses is of energy let loose, executive force invading, power in exercise, life demonstrated by activity."[1] How descriptive this is of the Holy Spirit and His work! And, as we will see, He is active today in the lives of believers and unbelievers alike.

I. What the Holy Spirit Is and Is Not

In some churches, the Holy Spirit is rarely mentioned, while in other congregations, He is made the center of attention. Both extremes have led to erroneous ideas concerning the person and work of God's Spirit. So let's turn to the Scriptures and consider what they say about the Holy Spirit in contrast to some false teachings regarding Him.

A. The Spirit is not an "it" but a person. Some people reject this idea. They think of the Holy Spirit as an impersonal force, a gaslike substance, or life principle.[2] The Bible, however, makes the truth clear. It attributes intelligence, understanding, and will to the Spirit . . . all of which are characteristics of rational beings (1 Cor. 2:10–11, 12:11). Its description of the Holy Spirit's activities also reveals His personhood. For instance, He creates, empowers, teaches, guides, intercedes, and comforts (Gen. 1:2, Job 33:4, Zech. 4:6, Luke 1:35, John 14:26, Acts 1:8, Rom. 8:26–27). Such evidence makes it plain that the Holy Spirit is indeed a person.

B. The Spirit is not passive but active and involved. Before Christ's betrayal and death, He told His disciples that His eventual departure would be to their advantage. For when He left, " 'the Helper' "—the Holy Spirit—would come to them (John 16:7). What would He do when He came? Jesus said that

---

1. J. I. Packer, *Keep In Step with the Spirit* (Old Tappan, N.J.: Fleming H. Revell Co., 1984), p. 57.

2. Walter Martin exposes many religious groups that deny the personal nature of the Holy Spirit in his book *The Kingdom of the Cults,* rev. ed. (Minneapolis, Minn.: Bethany House Publishers, 1985).

the Spirit would " 'convict the world concerning sin, and righteousness, and judgment,' " guide the disciples " 'into all truth,' " and glorify Christ (vv. 8, 13–14). Now that's involvement!

C. The Spirit is not imaginary but real and relevant. Seeing is believing—so goes the old adage. Underlying this saying is the assumption that what is real is visible; but this belief is not always valid. For example, we cannot see the wind, even though many of its effects are visible to us. Likewise, we cannot view the Holy Spirit with our eyes, but we can see the result of His work in our own lives and all over the world. Indeed, Jesus promised that after He ascended into heaven, the Holy Spirit would come and enable Christians to spread the gospel worldwide (Acts 1:8). This is being accomplished even today.

D. The Spirit is not less than God but fully God. The Holy Spirit is the Third Person of the Godhead. He is equal to the Father and the Son in every aspect of deity because He shares their divine essence. The Bible tells us this in numerous places, but perhaps the clearest passage is in Acts 5. Here the Apostle Peter confronts the deceit of Ananias and Sapphira. He asks Ananias, " 'Why has Satan filled your heart to lie to the Holy Spirit . . . ?' " (v. 3); then he adds, " 'You have not lied to men, but to God' " (v. 4b). Lying to the Holy Spirit is lying to deity, because the Spirit *is* God, no one less.

II. Why the Holy Spirit Is Here

On the eve of Christ's death, Jesus told His disciples that He would soon return to the Father (John 16:5)—also, that they would be despised and killed because of their commitment to Him (15:18–21, 16:2–3). These revelations grieved the disciples (16:6). They had expected Jesus to overthrow the Roman government and establish a world order of peace, prosperity, and justice (Luke 19:11, Acts 1:6; compare Isa. 9:2–7, 11:1–9). This belief was now shattered. Their king was going to leave them, and the coming of the new kingdom was now delayed. Realizing their sorrow, Christ sought to comfort them by telling them of a helper who would aid them more than He had been able to. How could this be so? Well, for one thing, the Holy Spirit could be present everywhere at once, whereas Jesus in His humanity could not because of the limitations of His body. Furthermore, the invisibility of the Spirit would help strengthen the disciples' faith. After all, it is usually easier to trust in what can be seen rather than in what cannot. But God often calls on us to place our faith in the invisible and the yet unfulfilled (John 20:29, Heb. 11), realizing that this is how our faith develops.

III. What the Holy Spirit Does

On that same fateful evening, Jesus went on to tell His disciples what the Holy Spirit would do once He came.

A. Among non-Christians. Jesus focused first on the Spirit's work in the lives of the unsaved. He said that God's Spirit would " 'convict the world concerning sin, . . . because they do not believe in Me' " (John 16:8–9). The Greek word translated *convict* "is a legal term that means to pronounce a judicial verdict by which the guilt of the culprit at the bar of justice is defined and fixed. The Spirit does not merely accuse men of sin, he brings to them an inescapable sense of guilt so that they realize their shame and helplessness before God."[3] To this Jesus added that the Spirit would convict the world of " 'righteousness, because I go to the Father, and you no longer behold Me' " (vv. 8, 10). The Holy Spirit acts as a divine prosecuting attorney, demonstrating to non-Christians that they do not measure up to God's perfect moral standard. Moreover, Jesus said that the Holy Spirit would convince the world " 'concerning judgment, because the ruler of this world has been judged' " (vv. 8, 11). Judgment is the logical consequence of standing guilty before God. Once people know that their thoughts and actions fall short of Christ's righteousness, a sense of condemnation follows. Even Satan, the wicked spiritual ruler of earth, realizes that his fate is sealed.

A Practical Word

Keeping in mind the Holy Spirit's activity of conviction can help relieve some of the stress many feel in evangelism. We who are Christians do not have to convince people that they are sinners. That's the job of God's Spirit. Instead, we have the joy of spreading good news. We get to proclaim that the solution to man's problem is personal faith in Christ, who is the bridge between sinful man and the holy God.

B. Among Christians. Jesus also promised that the Holy Spirit would guide believers further along the path of truth as it is embodied in Christ (vv. 13–15; compare 1:14, 14:6). One way the Spirit accomplished this was by inspiring the New Testament, the last written revelation of God to man. Today, the Holy Spirit illumines the content and application of the Scriptures, and He uses the Word and our circumstances to mature us into Christlikeness. In all these things, the Spirit's central goal is to glorify

3. Merrill C. Tenney, "The Gospel of John," in *The Expositor's Bible Commentary* (Grand Rapids, Mich.: Regency Reference Library, Zondervan Publishing House, 1981), vol. 9, p. 157.

Christ, not Himself (16:14). Those who make the Holy Spirit the primary focus of their lives or ministries are not getting support from Him. He magnifies the Son of God and empowers those who uplift the Son.

IV. How the Holy Spirit Is Felt

Reflecting on the identity and activity of the Holy Spirit, we can recognize at least four practical truths concerning His work in our lives.

A. Since He is a person, we feel Him as He heals relationships. The Spirit breaks through our walls, melts our hearts, and helps us piece together our broken bonds with people.

B. Since He is active and involved, we feel Him comforting us in our sorrows and guiding us in our pursuits. When He does this, He strengthens and molds us.

C. Since He is real and relevant, we feel Him giving us power and perseverance. As we submit to His work in our lives, He fills us and enables us to live as we should.

D. Since He is God, we feel Him as He controls our circumstances and transforms our lives. He is constantly at work, shaping us into vessels He can use for Christ's glory.

Living Insights

Study One

Paul had much to say about the power of the Holy Spirit in people's lives. Let's look at some of his remarks in his letters to the Galatians and the Ephesians.

• The following chart lists some key texts on the work of the Holy Spirit in the life of a believer. As you read the verses think in terms of: (1) what the Holy Spirit does and (2) what you should do as a result.

Continued on next page

The Spirit Who Is Not a Ghost	
What He Does	What I Should Do
Galatians 5:16–23	
Ephesians 1:13–14	
Ephesians 3:14–21	
Ephesians 5:15–21	

🌿 Living Insights

"Melt me. Mold me. Fill me. Use me."[4] Will you say these words to God? Will you allow yourself to be reshaped, refreshed, and renewed by His Holy Spirit? Inviting Him to carry out this process in your life will glorify Christ and help you discover a dimension of living you may have never known before.

- When it comes to relationships, will you ask the Lord to melt you?
- When it comes to objectives and the pursuit of His will, will you say "God, mold me"?
- As the days get long and the journey gets painful, will you beseech the Holy Spirit to fill you?
- As you face the circumstances that are upon you, will you tell the Lord you want Him to take control and use you?

---

4. "Spirit of the Living God," words and music by Daniel Iverson (Chicago, Ill.: Moody Press, 1963).

From Creation to Corruption

Genesis 1–5; Romans 3, 5, 6

"In the beginning God created the heavens and the earth" (Gen. 1:1). Although modern science was established by individuals who believed this verse,[1] the development of the Darwinian evolutionary theory eventually led the scientific community away from its biblical moorings. However, several recent discoveries are gradually causing scientists to reconsider the Bible's portrayal of the origin of the universe and life. For example, two of Britain's most distinguished scientists have argued that the chance of life arising from purely inorganic and natural processes is 1 in $10^{40,000}$—a number greater than the estimated number of atoms in the universe! In light of this, they have concluded that it must have taken divine intelligence to create life.[2] One of these scientists, Chandra Wickramasinghe, makes this assessment of evolution on the basis of his studies: "There's no evidence for any of the basic tenets of Darwinian evolution. I don't believe that there ever was any evidence for it. It was a social force that took over the world in 1860, and I think it has been a disaster for science ever since."[3]

Moving from biology to physics, we discover many astronomers who have concluded that the big bang theory strongly suggests, if not requires, the existence of a God who brought the universe into being from nothing. Astronomer and religious agnostic Robert Jastrow states the point this way: "Now we see how the astronomical evidence leads to a biblical view of the origin of the world. The details differ, but the essential elements in the astronomical and biblical accounts of Genesis are the same: the chain of events leading to man commenced suddenly and sharply at a definite moment in time, in a flash of light and energy."[4] These few examples show that once again, Genesis is earning the scientific respect it deserves. The focus of Genesis 1–3, however, is not as much on the origin of the universe as it is on the creation and corruption of man.

1. See "The Christian Doctrine of Creation and the Rise of Modern Natural Science," by G. E. Moore, in *Mind* 43 (1934), pp. 446–68; and *Maker of Heaven and Earth: A Study of the Christian Doctrine of Creation,* by Langdon Gilkey (Garden City, N.Y.: Doubleday and Co., 1959).

2. *Evolution from Space: A Theory of Cosmic Creationism,* by Fred Hoyle and N. C. Wickramasinghe (New York, N.Y.: Simon and Schuster, 1981).

3. Chandra Wickramasinghe, "Science and the Divine Origin of Life," in *The Intellectuals Speak Out about God: A Handbook for the Christian Student in a Secular Society,* ed. Roy Abraham Varghese (Chicago, Ill.: Regnery Gateway, 1984), pp. 30–31. For more on the controversies concerning the validity of Darwinian and neo-Darwinian evolution, see *The Post-Darwinian Controversies,* by James R. Moore (Cambridge, N.Y.: Cambridge University Press, 1979), and *Evolution: A Theory in Crisis,* by Michael Denton (Bethesda, Md.: Adler and Adler, 1985).

4. Robert Jastrow, *God and the Astronomers* (New York, N.Y.: W. W. Norton and Co., 1978), p. 14.

I. A Fresh Look at Our Roots

Let's get our bearings by examining Genesis 1:1–2:3 and then zeroing in on some significant facts it relates about man.

A. The literary structure. This passage uses a literary structure called *parallelism* to reveal basic information about the Creation. The section opens with a general statement about Creation, and the ensuing verses highlight the main Creation events. Verse 2 of chapter 1 tells us that "the earth was formless and void." The words *formless* and *void* are important, for the writer uses them, along with the term *day,* to present God's creative activity in a parallel form. This literary framework can be seen in the following chart:

The Six Days of Creation—Genesis 1	
The Formless Formed	The Void Filled
Day 1—Light and Dark (vv. 2–5)	Day 4—Lights of the Day and Night (vv. 14–19)
Day 2—Sea and Sky (vv. 6–8)	Day 5—Creatures of the Sea and Sky (vv. 20–23)
Day 3—Land and Vegetation (vv. 9–13)	Day 6—Creatures of the Land and Vegetation (vv. 24–31)

Notice that Day 1 corresponds to Day 4, Day 2 to Day 5, and Day 3 to Day 6. The writer wraps up his survey of Creation by focusing on the seventh day—the day God rested from His creative work (2:1–3).[5] With this narrative framework in mind, let's focus on some of the details given in this passage that relate directly to the creation of man.

B. Some significant details. Throughout Genesis 1, living things are created and told to reproduce "after their kind" (vv. 11–12, 21, 24–25). This phrase indicates that new life forms were created directly by God; they did not evolve from a common ancestor. These words also suggest that the creatures He made were distinct from one another and were created in a way that would maintain their uniqueness throughout all succeeding generations (compare 1 Cor. 15:39).[6] The same is true for man. Though he shares some characteristics with other creatures, he

5. An excellent discussion of the literary structure and interpretive problems of Genesis 1 is provided by Henri Blocher in his book *In the Beginning: The Opening Chapters of Genesis,* trans. David G. Preston (Downers Grove, Ill.: InterVarsity Press, 1984).

6. A scientific defense of this truth is given in *The Natural Limits to Biological Change,* by Lane P. Lester and Raymond G. Bohlin (Grand Rapids, Mich.: Zondervan Publishing House; Dallas, Tex.: Probe Ministries International, 1984).

differs from them in that he was created as the image of God (Gen. 1:26–27). Consequently, he alone was made to be God's visible representative and ruler on earth (vv. 27–28).[7]

II. How Corruption Began

Genesis 2:4–25 expands on what chapter 1 tells us about the creation of man. Here we learn that the first human being God made was male (v. 7). Verse 15 tells us that God placed this first man, Adam, in the Garden of Eden and told him to cultivate and keep it. Then "God commanded the man, saying, 'From any tree of the garden you may eat freely; but from the tree of the knowledge of good and evil you shall not eat, for in the day that you eat from it you shall surely die'" (vv. 16–17). Some time later the Lord made the first human female, Eve, and she and Adam lived together in complete innocence and intimacy (v. 25). Unfortunately, this beautiful scene eventually became ugly. Through the tragic abuse of their God-given freedom, Adam and Eve gave in to temptation and ate from the forbidden tree (3:1–6). What followed was exactly what God had warned—death. According to Scripture, death is separation. For example, when a person dies, his soul and spirit separate from his body (John 19:30, 2 Cor. 5:1–8). Although Adam and Eve did not experience immediate physical death, their sin initiated the degeneration process that would lead to their demise (Gen. 3:19). In other ways, they did experience separation right after they sinned. The open fellowship they had enjoyed with God was lost (v. 8). Their marital intimacy was also broken. No longer could they be in each other's presence "naked and unashamed" (2:25). They became preoccupied with themselves—hiding from each other in clothing and covering up their guilt by passing their blame to someone else (3:7, 9–13). Adam and Eve also forfeited their control over the earth. What had been submissive to their rule became a source of conflict and arduous labor (vv. 17–19). Corruption had indeed begun, and it would not remain confined to the Garden of Eden (vv. 23–24).

III. Where Corruption Leads

Adam and Eve were now depraved. This does not mean that they were as bad as they could be, but it does mean that they were as bad *off* as they could be. They were alienated from God, from the world they lived in, from each other, and even from themselves. Sin was polluting every aspect of their lives. And to make matters worse, Adam and Eve passed this disease on to their children. For instance,

---

7. Some helpful discussions on the meaning of God's image may be found in these materials: *In the Beginning,* by Blocher, chap. 4; *The Transforming Vision: Shaping a Christian World View,* by Brian J. Walsh and J. Richard Middleton, foreword by Nicholas Wolterstorff (Downers Grove, Ill.: InterVarsity Press, 1984); *Man: The Image of God,* by G. C. Berkouwer (Grand Rapids, Mich.: William B. Eerdmans Publishing Co., 1962).

one of their sons, Cain, manifested some of the symptoms of depravity when he maliciously murdered his brother Abel (4:1–8). Obviously, man, once the perfect image of God, was now bearing another image—that of sinful man. In fact, Genesis 5:3 specifically says that Adam's son Seth was conceived in the image of his father. Though man did not lose the divine image in which he was created (9:6, James 3:9), he now also represented himself and his depraved state. The rest of Scripture records the tragic march of corruption through much of human history. So pervasive and devastating did this disease become that the Apostle Paul wrote these words of universal condemnation:

Both Jews and Greeks are all under sin; as it is written,
"There is none righteous, not even one;
There is none who understands,
There is none who seeks for God;
All have turned aside, together they have be-
come useless;
There is none who does good,
There is not even one." (Rom. 3:9b–12)

IV. What This Means for Us

What is the bottom line? All of us are suffering from the same disease—depravity (3:23). Consequently, we are all experiencing the wages of sin—death (5:12, 6:23). Is there no escape? Are we all doomed? Not at all! God has mercifully provided a way out of corruption and into restored wholeness. What is it? The Apostle Paul tells us: "For if by the transgression of the one, death reigned through the one, much more those who receive the abundance of grace and of the gift of righteousness will reign in life through the One, Jesus Christ" (5:17). When we place our trust in Jesus Christ and His payment for our depravity, we are saved from the *penalty* of sin. As He changes us by the work of His Spirit, we begin to experience freedom from the *power* of sin. Finally, when we pass from this life and on to the other, we are saved from the *presence* of sin. Now that's a complete salvation from the corruption we experience daily! Unlike Humpty Dumpty, we can be put back together again because of all that Christ has done for us:

Jesus came to our wall;
Jesus Christ died for our fall.
He slew Queen Death.
He crushed King Sin.
Through grace He put us together again.[8]

8. Charles R. Swindoll, *Growing Deep in the Christian Life* (Portland, Oreg.: Multnomah Press, 1986), p. 211.

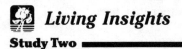

Living Insights

This study is giving us the opportunity to remember our roots. Reading what the Bible says about our beginning gives us insight that makes good sense.

● Genesis 1–4 records the beginning of our world. A good way to take a fresh look at our roots is to read these four chapters in a different version of the Bible than the one you are familiar with. Perhaps you'd like to try another translation—like King James, New King James, New American Standard, Revised Standard, New International—or a paraphrase, like the Living Bible. The key is to choose one that will give you a new perspective on these familiar verses.

Living Insights

Corruption is difficult to think about on a personal level. We don't like to dwell on our shortcomings. But we are better off by acknowledging our faults than by trying to cope with them in ignorance or secrecy. Realizing this, let's get personal about sin by answering the following questions.

Recognizing Corruption . . . Personally

What situations do I find tempting? _____

_____

_____

_____

_____

In what areas do I tend to hide from others? _____

_____

_____

_____

_____

When do I tend to blame others, refusing to take responsibility?

_____

_____

_____

_____

_____

Drawing on what I have learned in this study, how can I begin to over-come these moral weaknesses in my life?

_____

_____

_____

_____

_____

Exposing the Dark Side

Selected Scripture

Man was created as the image of the perfect God and placed in a beautiful garden in a trouble-free world. Yet man chose to disobey the One who gave him this environment to enjoy. In the wake of his sin came depravity and death. Looking back, we see the litter this decision has thrown onto the path of human history. Hostility, greed, envy, deceit, bigotry, violence ... these are all products of man's dark side. Lest we try to ignore or downplay our condition, God has inspired and preserved a record that exposes it for what it is—evil. Mercifully, however, He has not only unveiled our disease but also provided the cure. In this lesson, we will explore in greater depth both our basic problem and God's gracious solution.

I. Depravity Defined and Explained

Before going any further, we need to better understand the nature and extent of depravity.

A. What is depravity? The Bible describes man's depraved condition in a variety of ways. For instance, it tells us that man is: enslaved to sin and needs to be set free (Luke 4:18, John 8:31–36, Rom. 6:16–18); sick with sin and in need of healing (Mark 2:17); and impoverished by sin and needs God's riches (Luke 4:18, 2 Cor. 8:9, Eph. 2:7). The Scriptures also say that man is: polluted by sin and needs to be cleansed (Mark 7:14–23, Eph. 5:25–27, Titus 1:15, 1 John 1:7–9); blinded by sin and needs restored sight (Luke 4:18, 2 Cor. 4:3–6); lost in sin's darkness and needs Christ's light (John 8:12, 12:35); and dead in sin and needs new life (Eph. 2:1–6, Col. 2:13). These descriptions show that depravity is a degenerative disease. Those who have it suffer corruption physically, emotionally, mentally, spiritually, and relationally. Furthermore, they cannot eradicate this sickness from their lives. Once they catch it, they have it for a lifetime.

B. What is depravity's extent? Scripture tells us that depravity affects all of us, in every aspect of our nature. It shows us that we are in need of being purified entirely (1 Thess. 5:23) and that all human beings are corrupt, not just some (Eccles. 7:20, 29; Rom. 3:9–18, 23). We caught the disease of depravity from our parents, they from their parents, and so on, back to Adam and Eve. David remorsefully expressed this during a time of unguarded confession to the Lord: "Behold, I was brought forth in [a state of] iniquity; my mother was sinful who conceived me [and I, too, am sinful]" (Ps. 51:5).[1] Like David, we are all unable

---

1. The Amplified Bible, as quoted by Charles R. Swindoll in *Growing Deep in the Christian Life* (Portland, Oreg.: Multnomah Press, 1986), p. 216.

to please God by our own efforts. Without His grace—His un-
merited favor—we are doomed to an earthly life of death and an
everlasting life of darkness, misery, and destruction (Matt. 7:13,
13:49; 2 Thess. 1:7–9; Rev. 21:8).

II. Humanity Surveyed and Exposed

Scripture is filled with examples of human depravity. Let's look at
the portraits of five men who show us the good and the bad sides
of human nature.

A. Noah. Some time after man's fall from innocence, "the Lord
saw that the wickedness of man was great on the earth, and
that every intent of the thoughts of his heart was only evil
continually" (Gen. 6:5). So God decided to clear the earth of
man, beast, and fowl through a great flood (vv. 7, 17). However,
there was one man who was faithful to the Lord—Noah (vv. 8–9).
God chose to spare him, his family, and some male and female
animals of each species (vv. 17–20). Their lives were preserved
in a huge ark Noah built according to the Lord's specifications
(vv. 14–16). After the rain stopped and the flood waters sub-
sided, Noah and his companions left the ark and stepped into
a world free of sin—or so they thought. "Noah began farming
and planted a vineyard. And he drank of the wine and became
drunk, and uncovered himself inside his tent" (9:20–21). Why did
Noah—a godly man—commit such an indecent act? Because
he had a depraved nature. That's the reason many otherwise
faithful people fall into sin today. Like the rest of us, they are still
plagued by the disease called depravity. Realizing this should
not only humble us but help us avoid placing others on pedes-
tals. Godly people certainly deserve our respect, but none of
them are worthy of our worship.

B. Moses. One of the greatest saints in all Scripture is Moses. He
was mightily used by God to lead the Hebrew people out of their
slavery in Egypt (Exod. 5–14). He was the man God chose to
receive the Law and unveil it to the Hebrews (19–31). He was
the one who led God's chosen people through the wilderness,
even though they often assaulted him verbally (15:27–17:7,
Num. 11–14). And yet, Moses was not without a dark side. For
example, when he was about forty years old, he murdered a
man in an attempt to enact his own plan of deliverance for the
Hebrews (Exod. 2:11–12, Acts 7:25–28). Forty years later, he
resisted God's call to be His spokesman to Pharoah and the
Hebrews (Exod. 3:1–4:17). Moreover, during an outbreak of
complaints among the Hebrews, Moses chose to disregard God's
way of handling the problem and instead responded in a fit of

rage (Num. 20:2–12). Again and again, this man of God demonstrated that he was also a victim of depravity.

C. David. Many years after the Hebrews entered the Promised Land, God reached out and chose a young shepherd named David to reign as king over His people (Ps. 78:70–71). The Bible calls David "a man after [God's] own heart" (1 Sam. 13:14; compare Acts 13:22). He "shepherded [the Israelites] according to the integrity of his heart, / And guided them with his skillful hands" (Ps. 78:72). In fact, for the first time in her history, Israel rose to economic, military, and spiritual prominence under David's rule. But as great as David was, he still had feet of clay. One fateful evening, he took a walk on his palace roof and saw a beautiful woman bathing (2 Sam. 11:2). With his heart full of lust, he sent for her and "lay with her" (vv. 3–4a). Bathsheba, the woman he had violated, became pregnant (v. 5). Desperate to cover his tracks, David engineered the death of Uriah, Bathsheba's husband (vv. 14–25), so that Bathsheba could become his wife (v. 27). Adultery, deceit, and murder—all sinful acts committed by a believer. Why? Because he was depraved.

D. Peter. Turning to the New Testament, we find a hard-working fisherman named Peter, who gave up his trade to follow Christ. One of his greatest moments was when he identified Jesus as " 'the Christ, the Son of the living God' " (Matt. 16:16). But at Jesus' most difficult hour, Peter deserted, denied, and cursed Him (26:47–56, 69–74). Another faithful follower had fallen prey to the corruption within.

E. Paul. Perhaps the most well-known evangelist, church planter, writer, and theologian of the early Church was the Apostle Paul. And yet, he openly admitted his struggle with sin. As you read his words, reflect on your own inward struggles.

> I do not understand what I do. For what I want to do I do not do, but what I hate I do. And if I do what I do not want to do, I agree that the law is good. As it is, it is no longer I myself who do it, but it is sin living in me. I know that nothing good lives in me, that is, in my sinful nature. For I have the desire to do what is good, but I cannot carry it out. For what I do is not the good I want to do; no, the evil I do not want to do—this I keep on doing." (Rom. 7:15–19)[2]

Like Paul, we may sincerely desire to please God, but even our best wishes and intentions can be thwarted by the depravity that lurks within us all.

---

2. *The NIV Study Bible* (Grand Rapids, Mich.: Zondervan Bible Publishers, 1985).

III. One Great Exception

Although the lives we have seen paint a terribly bleak picture, all is not hopeless. For one man broke the awful progression of depravity. The Son of God took on a perfect human nature and lived a life in complete obedience to the Father. Then He, who never committed a single sin, paid the penalty for *our* sin by dying on the cross in our place. By trusting in Him as our Savior, we can receive forgiveness for our wrongdoing and power to overcome sin (Rom. 7:24–8:39, 1 John 1:5–10). That's great news!

IV. Two Available Options

When we boil down all that we've learned, we are faced with two options. *We can choose to live either as victims of our depravity or as victors through Jesus Christ's power.* We do not have to give in to our evil inclinations (Rom. 6:12–19, James 1:12–18), but we cannot fight them successfully on our own. Only in Christ can we live victoriously. Which option will you choose?

Living Insights

Study One

We've covered a large chunk of doctrine so far . . . and we're only at the halfway mark! Let's take a midterm break and review some of the truths we've already gleaned.

- Using your study guide and Bible, look back through the first twelve lessons. Try to pinpoint one *truth* from each study that stands out as important to you and write it in the space provided. It may be something new, or perhaps it's something previously learned but presented in a fresh way.

GROWING DEEP IN THE CHRISTIAN LIFE
Doctrine and Discernment

The Value of Knowing the Scoop _____

_____

_____

_____

Don't Forget to Add a Cup of Discernment _____

_____

_____

Continued on next page

The Bible

God's Book—God's Voice _____

_____

_____

_____

Handling the Scriptures Accurately _____

_____

_____

_____

God the Father

Knowing God: Life's Major Pursuit _____

_____

_____

_____

Loving God: Our Ultimate Response _____

_____

_____

_____

The Lord Jesus Christ

Mary's Little Lamb _____

_____

_____

_____

When the God-Man Walked among Us _____

_____

_____

_____

Changing Lives Is Jesus' Business _____

_____

_____

_____

The Holy Spirit

The Spirit Who Is Not a Ghost _____

_____

_____

_____

The Depravity of Humanity

From Creation to Corruption _____

_____

_____

_____

Exposing the Dark Side _____

_____

_____

_____

 Living Insights

Study Two ▪▪

We hope this series of studies is teaching you theology's great truths *and* its great practicality. Are you applying what you've been learning? Let's find out.

- The following exercise is identical to the one in our previous study, with one change. Here you are to review each lesson to find one *application* you feel is significant to that particular study.

Continued on next page

GROWING DEEP IN THE CHRISTIAN LIFE
Doctrine and Discernment

The Value of Knowing the Scoop _____

_____

_____

_____

Don't Forget to Add a Cup of Discernment _____

_____

_____

_____

The Bible

God's Book—God's Voice _____

_____

_____

_____

Handling the Scriptures Accurately _____

_____

_____

_____

God the Father

Knowing God: Life's Major Pursuit _____

_____

_____

_____

Loving God: Our Ultimate Response _____

_____

_____

_____

The Lord Jesus Christ

Mary's Little Lamb _____

_____

_____

_____

When the God-Man Walked among Us _____

_____

_____

_____

Changing Lives Is Jesus' Business _____

_____

_____

_____

The Holy Spirit

The Spirit Who Is Not a Ghost _____

_____

_____

_____

The Depravity of Humanity

From Creation to Corruption _____

_____

_____

_____

Exposing the Dark Side _____

_____

_____

_____

"Mr. Smith, Meet Your Substitute"
Romans 3

A substitute is someone who takes the place of or acts instead of another. In the classroom, a substitute teacher instructs the students when their regular teacher is absent. In baseball, a substitute hitter or runner is sometimes used to maximize a team's chances of winning. Even in the political or corporate arenas, the vice president may sometimes carry out the president's duties. What is true in education, sports, politics, and business is true in the spiritual realm as well. We need a substitute who will act on our behalf before God. Why do we need a substitute? What kind of substitute do we need? How can this substitute become our personal representative? These are the questions we are going to answer in this lesson. They will take us to the heart of the Bible's doctrine of salvation.

I. Four Major Issues

Did you know that a portion of your biography is in the Bible? In fact, all human beings can find themselves in Scripture. One book that reveals some of our deepest secrets is Romans. And the passage in this epistle that bares this information so clearly and succinctly is chapter 3. Here four crucial issues are discussed and applied in relation to our standing before God. Regardless of who we are, we will find ourselves described in this text.

A. Our condition: totally depraved. The first issue we see unveiled is our complete depravity:

> Both Jews and Greeks are all under sin;
> as it is written,
>> "Their throat is an open grave,
>> With their tongues they keep deceiving,"
>> "The poison of asps is under their lips";
>> "Whose mouth is full of cursing and bitterness";
>> "Their feet are swift to shed blood,
>> Destruction and misery are in their paths,
>> And the path of peace have they not known."
>> "There is no fear of God before their eyes."
> (Rom. 3:9–10a, 13–18)

That's not a pretty picture, is it? But it is a realistic portrait of each one of us. We are sinners through and through. If depravity were colored blue, we would be blue inside and out. Our natures, thoughts, emotions, words, and behavior would all have a blue tinge. Of course, depravity does not preclude our ability to do good things, for even Jesus said that evil people know how to give good gifts to their loved ones (Matt. 7:11a). But the good we can do is totally inadequate for setting things right with God. Further study in Romans 3 shows us why this is so.

B. God's character: infinitely holy. The standard by which our lives are measured is the Lord's perfect character. Notice how this truth is stated in Romans: "The righteousness of God has been manifested, . . . even the righteousness of God through faith in Jesus Christ for all those who believe; for there is no distinction; for all have sinned and fall short of the glory of God" (3:21–23). We can't begin to compare ourselves to the Lord's absolute holiness and purity. He is purer than freshly fallen snow; we are as dirty as mud-soaked clothing. Consequently, there is no way we, in our sinful condition, can match the Lord's untainted holiness.

C. Our need: a substitute. This biblical revelation of our condition leaves no doubt—we are in desperate need of a substitute. We need someone who can pay our debt—death (6:23)—and clean us out so that we can be found blameless according to the Lord's morally perfect standard. Of course, our substitute would have to be uninfected by the disease of depravity. Indeed, He would have to measure up to God's holiness in every way, while remaining like us in humanity so that He could die for us. In other words, He would have to be deity as well as a morally perfect man both by nature and by choice. Do we have such a substitute? Thankfully, yes!

D. God's provision: a Savior. God has provided a way for us to be "justified freely by his grace through the redemption that came by Christ Jesus" (3:24).[1] The Lord has done this by presenting Jesus "as a sacrifice of atonement, through faith in his blood. He did this to demonstrate his justice, because in his forbearance he had left the sins committed beforehand unpunished—he did it to demonstrate his justice at the present time, so as to be just and the one who justifies those who have faith in Jesus" (vv. 25–26).[2] The key word in these verses is *justified*. It does not mean "just as if I had never sinned," for the Lord knows that we are dead in sin and in need of new life. However, justification does stand for the act whereby God declares righteous the believing sinner while he is still in his sinning state. We can get a handle on this idea by imagining a courtroom scene with God as the judge and us as the accused. The Lord looks down on us and asks, "Have you loved Me with all your being?" Ashamed, we look up at Him and answer, "No, Your Honor." Next He asks, "Have you loved others as you have loved yourself?"

1. *The NIV Study Bible* (Grand Rapids, Mich.: Zondervan Bible Publishers, 1985).

2. *The NIV Study Bible.*

Again we answer in the negative. Finally, He asks, "Do you believe you are sinners, and do you trust in My Son's payment for your sin?" This time we respond positively, "Yes, Your Honor." Then we hear the amazing words of grace falling from God's lips: "Since My Son, Jesus Christ, has paid for your debt and you have accepted His payment, you are hereby fully pardoned."[3] Does this scene give any hint that we have earned our salvation? None at all! Christ has done the work; all we must do is receive His merciful payment for our sin. Romans 4:4–5 says it well: "Now to the one who works, his wage is not reckoned as a favor, but as what is due. But to the one who does not work, but believes in Him who justifies the ungodly, his faith is reckoned as righteousness." We can have our sins forgiven and inherit everlasting life if we will simply place our trust in our substitute—the perfect God-man, Jesus Christ.

Spiritual Cleaning Provided

The scarlet letter of sin stains our garments, branding us guilty and alienating us from God. Like the murderous Lady Macbeth, futilely trying to rub the stains of guilt away, we are helpless to make ourselves clean. We may cry out with her, "Out, damned spot!" but regardless of our fervent efforts, the stain will remain. Only with the Lord is there cleansing:

> If we confess our sins, He is faithful and righteous to forgive us our sins and to *cleanse* us from all unrighteousness. (1 John 1:9, emphasis added)

No matter how obvious the stain or how deeply it has sunk into the fabric of our being, God's forgiveness can remove it entirely and make us pure:

> "Though your sins are as scarlet,
> They will be as white as snow;
> Though they are red like crimson,
> They will be like wool." (Isa. 1:18)

Is your life a bloody garment of sin—spotted a dark crimson from the dried stains of past sins or bright scarlet from those freshly committed? Only the Lord can clean these kind of stains. And when He does, your life will be the whitest of whites—like newly fallen snow or virgin wool.

---

3. This courtroom illustration is a revised form of one that is used by Billy Graham in his book *How to Be Born Again* (Waco, Tex.: Word Books, 1977), pp. 118–21.

II. Three Crucial Questions

Now that we all have been exposed for who we are—depraved human beings in need of Christ the Lord—let's consider three essential questions and their biblical answers. This will help crystalize the teaching of Romans 3.

A. Is there any hope for lost sinners? Yes—Christ! Not Christ and a local church, not Christ and good works, not Christ and sincerity, not Christ and water baptism...*Christ alone* is necessary for salvation. Only His death on the cross and His resurrection from the grave are sufficient to rescue us from the death grip of sin. As Jesus said, "'I am *the* way, and *the* truth, and *the* life; no one comes to the Father, but through Me'" (John 14:6, emphasis added). The Apostle Peter echoed these words when he declared, "'There is salvation in no one else [but Christ]; for there is no other name under heaven that has been given among men, by which we must be saved'" (Acts 4:12).

B. Isn't there any work for a seeker to do? No—just believe! Salvation is a gift from God; we cannot earn it and do not deserve it. To receive this gift, all we must do is accept it willingly.[4] Besides, assuming that good works could save us, how much work would we have to do to satisfy a holy, perfect God? Obviously, since we are sinners by nature, we could never do enough to measure up to God's morally pure standard. Fortunately, however, God has done it for us by implementing a salvation plan that calls for faith, not works, on our part.

C. Is there any way for the saved to lose the gift of salvation? No—never! Since salvation is a gift received, not a wage earned, we can never lose it once we accept it. It doesn't make any difference how often or how seriously we disobey the Lord after we're saved. Because we didn't have to be good enough to receive God's gift, we can't become bad enough to lose it. In fact, it was when we were wallowing in our sin, fighting against the Lord, that He stooped down and, out of His superabundant love, offered us complete forgiveness in Christ (Rom. 5:6–8,

---

4. Some people think that the act of faith is a work if it precedes conversion. Therefore, they conclude that first God saves us; then, He gives us the ability to believe in Christ as our Savior. The basic problem with this position is that it is built on a mistaken premise; namely, that placing faith in Jesus is a work. The Bible clearly states that the act of faith is a means of *accepting* the gift of salvation, not a means of *earning* the gift (Rom. 3:27–28; 5:1–2, 6–11; Gal. 3:2–14). An impoverished beggar who's offered one million dollars does not earn this gift by reaching out his hand to accept it. Likewise, we who have been impoverished by sin do not earn God's abundant, undeserved riches in Christ by simply receiving them. We are saved by means of, not on the basis of, our faith.

1 John 4:10). How could we ever become worse than when we were enemies of God?[5]

III. Two Possible Responses

Given what we have learned in this study, we have only two ways to go. We can either believe in Christ and accept the gift of salvation or not believe in Christ and refuse the gift of salvation. There is no third choice—no neutral stance. Either we are Christians or we are not Christians; either we have everlasting life or we face everlasting death.

IV. One Final Reminder

Our choices are clear, and so is at least one other factor—we do not have forever to accept Christ as Savior. One day, probably unexpectedly, death will overtake us. At that moment, the choice we made on earth regarding Christ will be unalterable for eternity. What is your relationship to Jesus Christ? Have you believed in Him and thereby secured everlasting life? If not, we who are believers "beg you on behalf of Christ, be reconciled to God" by placing your faith in Jesus today (2 Cor. 5:20).

Living Insights

Study One

After two lessons on man's totally depraved nature, a study on God's salvation plan is like a cool breeze on a hot day! The doctrine of Christ as our substitute is of special importance to all believers.

- The Gospel of John is filled with marvelous word pictures describing our salvation; Jesus had many occasions to illustrate His substitutionary deliverance while He was on earth. Read the following passages, and then elaborate on what Christ meant by the pictures He presented.

Salvation in the Gospel of John

The Living Water—John 4:1–45

_____

_____

_____

5. Some materials that address the hard-to-understand passages related to eternal security are: *Growing Up in God's Family*, ed. Bill Watkins, from the Bible-teaching ministry of Charles R. Swindoll (Fullerton, Calif.: Insight for Living, 1986), p. 57; *Once Saved, Always Saved*, by R. T. Kendall (Chicago, Ill.: Moody Press, 1983); and *Major Bible Themes*, rev. ed., by Lewis Sperry Chafer (Grand Rapids, Mich.: Zondervan Publishing House, 1974), chap. 33.

The Bread of Life—John 6:22–65

_____

_____

_____

The Resurrection and the Life—John 11:1–53

_____

_____

_____

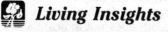 *Living Insights*

Study Two ▬▬▬▬▬▬▬▬▬▬▬▬▬▬▬▬▬▬▬▬▬▬

The doctrine of salvation has been expressed musically down through church history. This is easily observed by taking a look at practically any hymnal or chorus book.

- Locate a hymnal or chorus book. List all the songs that refer to salvation somewhere in the lyrics. Your list should be quite lengthy in a rather short time. Chances are you'll find a favorite song in that list—feel free to go right ahead and *sing!*

Songs of Salvation

_____

_____

_____

_____

_____

_____

_____

_____

_____

_____

The Remedy for Our Disease

Isaiah 53, Leviticus, Hebrews

Christians appear to be people centered around the cross on which Jesus died. They often put large crosses on their churches and set small ones on their altars. Many believers wear crosses around their necks; some even wear cross-shaped earrings. Several of the best-loved hymns of the Christian Church are about Jesus' cross: "Lift High the Cross," "The Old Rugged Cross," "At the Cross," and "Am I a Soldier of the Cross?" On the surface, this preoccupation with a symbol of death is gruesome. After all, the ancient Roman practice of crucifixion was one of the most humiliating and painful ways to die.[1] And in light of the scourging Jesus endured just before His crucifixion, the image of the cross seems even more hideous.[2] Why do Christians have this apparently macabre attraction? First of all, their interest is not in the cross itself but in what it represents—the death of Jesus Christ. And second, their absorption with Christ's death does not indicate a sick obsession with His crucifixion but shows a vivid awareness of its significance. The cross on which Jesus hung was only a piece of wood, yet the One who died on that cross was being punished for the sins of every human being. The cross, therefore, stands for what the Savior did for mankind. But why did He have to shed His blood to pay for our wrongs? The answer is rooted in the Old Testament practice of animal sacrifice. As we examine this ancient ritual, we will see its significance to the death of Jesus—the remedy for our disease.

I. A Prediction of the Substitute

Before delving into the biblical record regarding animal sacrifices, let's look at what Isaiah predicted about Christ and His suffering on our behalf.

A. His appearance, our rejection. Unlike many movie portrayals of Jesus, Isaiah says that Christ "had no beauty or majesty to attract us to him, / nothing in his appearance that we should desire him" (Isa. 53:2b).[3] He was a plain-looking Jew—no visible aura surrounded Him, and no halo floated above Him. "He was [also] despised and forsaken of men, / A man of sorrows, and acquainted with grief; / And like one from whom men hide their face, / He was despised, and we did not esteem Him" (v. 3). We

1. See *The Trial and Death of Jesus Christ,* by James Stalker (Grand Rapids, Mich.: Academie Books, Zondervan Publishing House, 1983), pp. 95–96.

2. In their book *Verdict on the Shroud: Evidence for the Death and Resurrection of Jesus Christ* (Ann Arbor, Mich.: Servant Books, 1981), Kenneth Stevenson and Gary Habermas provide some excellent historical and medical material on the physical sufferings of Christ and how they compare to the image in the Shroud of Turin.

3. *The NIV Study Bible* (Grand Rapids, Mich.: Zondervan Bible Publishers, 1985).

know from the Gospels that many people followed Jesus during His earthly ministry. However, those same records tell us that in His hour of deepest need, even His closest followers deserted Him, leaving Him to be tried, tormented, tortured, and crucified alone (Matt. 26:47–27:50, Mark 14:43–15:37, Luke 22:47–23:46, John 18:1–19:30). Jesus came to rescue people from sin, but they turned their backs on Him.

B. His work, our salvation. Ironically, man's rejection of Christ led to the foundation of our salvation—His death. Notice how Isaiah states it:

> Surely our griefs He Himself bore,
> And our sorrows He carried;
> Yet we ourselves esteemed Him stricken,
> Smitten of God, and afflicted.
> But He was pierced through for our transgressions,
> He was crushed for our iniquities;
> The chastening for our well-being fell upon Him,
> And by His scourging we are healed.
> All of us like sheep have gone astray,
> Each of us has turned to his own way;
> But the Lord has caused the iniquity of us all
> To fall on Him. (Isa. 53:4–6)

As these verses indicate, Jesus' physical suffering was great. But the pain He felt in His body was nothing compared to the agony He experienced in His soul. The Holy One, who had never sinned, bore the sin of all mankind. And in that awful moment, the love that had flowed for an eternity between Jesus and His Father was temporarily cut off. Jesus was so deeply wounded by this severance that He screamed in despair, *"Eli, Eli, lama sabachthani?"*— "My God, My God, why hast Thou forsaken Me?" (Matt. 27:46). Certainly, no one but Christ has ever paid as high a price for another's deliverance.

II. An Explanation of the Sacrifice

Knowing Jesus died for our sins is not the same as knowing why He had to die for them. The answer is found in Leviticus, where we learn about the animal sacrifices performed by the Hebrews to restore broken fellowship with God. Let's take a look at this religious practice and consider how it relates to Christ's death on the cross.

A. Animal sacrifice. In Bible times, when a wrong was committed, the person responsible brought an unblemished animal to the altar as an offering for the sin (Lev. 4:1–3). Then the wrongdoer or the priest laid a hand on the animal's head—an act that symbolized the transfer of guilt from the offender to the innocent animal (v. 4). With this exchange complete, the priest killed the animal, sprinkling some of its blood on one side of the altar and pouring the remainder of its blood at the altar's base (5:5–9). The emphasis on blood was important, as God revealed: " ' "The life of the flesh is in the blood, and I have given it to you on the altar to make atonement for your souls; for it is the blood by reason of the life that makes atonement" ' " (17:11). The Hebrew word for *atonement* means "cover." God was saying that the blood would cover the sin, putting it out of sight and bringing "at-one-ment," or peace, between the sinner and the Lord. Animal sacrifice was a common occurrence in ancient Israel. Consequently, it was a stark reminder to the people that they were sinners and in continual need of being reconciled to God.

B. Christ's sacrifice. The writer of the Epistle to the Hebrews used the everyday sight of animal sacrifices to shed profound light on Jesus' sacrifice. He points out the difference, however, observing that the frequent slaying of animals as sin offerings demonstrated that their blood was insufficient to take away sins permanently (Heb. 10:1, 3–4). "Otherwise, would they not have ceased to be offered, because the worshipers, having once been cleansed, would no longer have had consciousness of sins?" (v. 2). Therefore, a better sacrifice was needed—one that could remove sin from people forever. This sacrifice was provided by Christ. When He shed His blood on the cross, He died "for sins for all time" (v. 12a; compare v. 10). The Father has accepted Christ's death as sufficient payment for human sin; He has looked at our debt through the sacrifice of His Son and stamped it PAID. When we trust in Jesus as our Savior, our debt is canceled forever (Col. 2:13–14). That's why Christ had to shed His blood.

III. Our Response to the Savior

The spotless Lamb of God allowed our sins to be transferred to Him. By this, He could offer us complete and final atonement. As Paul explains, "He [the Father] made Him [the Son] who knew no sin to be sin on our behalf, that we might become the righteousness of God in Him" (2 Cor. 5:21). Once we place our faith in Jesus, we are reconciled to God—for now and always. If you have not taken this step of faith, the Lord urges you to do so now. If you have already accepted Christ as your Savior, take some time now to thank Him for dying in your place, and remember:

> While we were yet sinners, Christ died for us. Much more then, having now been justified by His blood, we shall be saved from the wrath of God through Him. For if while we were enemies, we were reconciled to God through the death of His Son, much more, having been reconciled, we shall be saved by His life. And not only this, but we also

exult in God through our Lord Jesus Christ, through whom we have now received the reconciliation. (Rom. 5:8b–11)

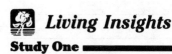 *Living Insights*

Study One ▬▬▬▬▬▬▬▬▬▬▬▬▬▬▬▬▬▬▬▬▬▬▬▬▬▬▬▬▬▬▬▬

So much of this study revolves around the powerful fifty-third chapter of Isaiah. Let's camp there for a little while . . . it will be a profitable study, guaranteed!

● Reread Isaiah 53 and list twenty of the chapter's *key words*. With the assistance of a good Bible dictionary, come up with a working definition for each term. Conclude by writing a statement about the word's significance to the message of the text.

Isaiah 53

Key Word: _____

Definition: _____   Significance: _____

_____   _____

_____   _____

Key Word: _____

Definition: _____   Significance: _____

_____   _____

_____   _____

Key Word: _____

Definition: _____   Significance: _____

_____   _____

_____   _____

Key Word: _____

Definition: _____   Significance: _____

_____   _____

_____   _____

Continued on next page

105

Key Word: _____

Definition: _____   Significance: _____

_____   _____

_____   _____

Key Word: _____

Definition: _____   Significance: _____

_____   _____

_____   _____

Key Word: _____

Definition: _____   Significance: _____

_____   _____

_____   _____

Key Word: _____

Definition: _____   Significance: _____

_____   _____

_____   _____

Key Word: _____

Definition: _____   Significance: _____

_____   _____

_____   _____

Key Word: _____

Definition: _____   Significance: _____

_____   _____

_____   _____

Key Word: _____

Definition: _____   Significance: _____

_____   _____

_____   _____

Key Word: _____

Definition: _____   Significance: _____

_____   _____

_____   _____

Key Word: _____

Definition: _____   Significance: _____

_____   _____

_____   _____

Key Word: _____

Definition: _____   Significance: _____

_____   _____

_____   _____

Key Word: _____

Definition: _____   Significance: _____

_____   _____

_____   _____

Key Word: _____

Definition: _____   Significance: _____

_____   _____

_____   _____

Key Word: _____

Definition: _____   Significance: _____

_____   _____

_____   _____

Key Word: _____

Definition: _____   Significance: _____

_____   _____

Continued on next page

Key Word: _____

Definition: _____   Significance: _____

_____   _____

_____   _____

Key Word: _____

Definition: _____   Significance: _____

_____   _____

_____   _____

Living Insights

There is nothing more exciting than the story of how a person came to know Jesus Christ. We all enjoy learning about the process that led another brother or sister to discover Jesus, the remedy for their disease.

- When's the last time you read a Christian biography? This study provides an excellent occasion to learn the testimony of someone else's salvation. Visit a Christian bookstore or church library and pick up a copy of a life story that interests you. If you're stuck, try *Born Again* by Charles Colson, *Surprised by Joy* by C. S. Lewis, or the fictional account of a man's conversion as told in the wonderful novel *Johnny Come Home* by R. C. Sproul.

His Coming Is Sure . . . Are You?

Selected Scripture

So far in our study of Christian doctrine, we have seen that at the right time in history, the Son of God joined Himself to human flesh in the womb of the virgin Mary. After living a sinless life, He was betrayed, executed, and buried—but death could not hold Him down. On the third day, He rose from the grave in a glorified human body that can never decay or die. Yet, He did not remain on earth. Forty days after His resurrection, He ascended into heaven. Will He ever return bodily to our planet? The Scriptures answer with a resounding yes! The Lord *is* coming again; there's no doubt about it. We will use this lesson to survey what the New Testament says about this momentous event and how we should respond to it.

I. Extremes That Block Our Balance

Mention Christ's return and you will likely get any number of reactions, most of which can be grouped into three categories: fanatical intensity, theological ignorance, and biblical balance.

A. Fanatical intensity. Some people "go nuts" when the subject of Christ's return comes up. They see signs of His coming in practically every newspaper article, current event, and calamity. They are so preoccupied with His predicted bodily reentry that they have lost nearly all interest in the here and now. Consequently, they often become irresponsible on the job, in the home, and at the church. Sometimes they even set a specific date for Christ's return and encourage others to join them in a twenty-four-hour-a-day heavenly watch. This response is never condoned in Scripture. We should certainly live in joyful anticipation of the Lord's arrival, but it should not keep us from living responsibly and productively in the present.

B. Theological ignorance. Other people hear about Christ's return . . . and yawn. To them, the subject has no practical significance or immediate urgency. After all, Jesus left the earth almost two thousand years ago, and He may not return for two thousand more. Therefore, they conclude, we need to get on with today's business and lay aside tomorrow's issues. Like the response of fanatical intensity, this one is also unbiblical and misguided. It's true that Christ may not return for many years to come. On the other hand, He may come back today. Keeping this in mind will help us remain alert for His coming while staying involved in today's needs.

Needed: Biblical Balance

Between the extremes of fanatical intensity and theological ignorance lies biblical balance. We need to be informed

---

about Christ's return, believing it could occur at any moment while living as if it will not happen for another two or three generations. Of course, some people think it's foolish to look forward to a promised event that has not been fulfilled for almost two millennia. But their faulty judgment should not deter us from hoping in Christ's coming. As the Apostle Peter says:

> Do not let this one fact escape your notice, beloved, that with the Lord one day is as a thousand years, and a thousand years as one day. The Lord is not slow about His promise, as some count slowness, but is patient toward you, not wishing for any to perish but for all to come to repentance. (2 Pet. 3:8–9)

Don't mistake the Lord's current patience for permanent absence. He is coming back, so we'd better get ready.

II. Facts That Confirm Our Conviction

A close study of the Bible shows that the return of Jesus Christ holds a prominent place in God's program. For example, one out of every thirty verses of Scripture mentions either Christ's return or events directly related to it. The New Testament alone contains 318 references to His coming again. In fact, only four of the New Testament's twenty-seven books do not mention it. Turning to the Old Testament, one can find the subject addressed by Job, Moses, David, Isaiah, Jeremiah, and most of the minor prophets. Jesus' return is so important in Scripture that it comes up "twice as much as the atonement, and eight times as much as Christ's first coming."[1]

III. Predictions That Affirm Our Assurance

Let's briefly look into some passages of Scripture that speak about Jesus' imminent return.

A. Matthew 24:42–44. On one occasion Jesus was asked, " 'What will be the sign of Your coming, and of the end of the age?' " (v. 3b). In the midst of His lengthy answer, He said,

> "Be on the alert, for you do not know which day your Lord is coming. But be sure of this, that if the head of the house had known at what time of the night the thief was coming, he would have been on the alert and would not have allowed his house to be broken into. For this reason you be ready too; for the Son of

---

1. William M. Arnett, "The Second Coming: Millennial Views," in *Basic Christian Doctrines*, ed. Carl F. H. Henry (1962; reprint, Grand Rapids, Mich.: Baker Book House, 1971), p. 278.

Man is coming at an hour when you do not think He will." (vv. 42–44)

Although Jesus said that His return will occur at an unexpected time, He assured His followers that it *will* take place. Therefore, we always need to be alert and prepared.

B. Mark 8:38. Another time Christ told His disciples, " 'Whoever is ashamed of Me and My words in this adulterous and sinful generation, the Son of Man will also be ashamed of him when He comes in the glory of His Father with the holy angels.' " Here Jesus confirms that His coming again is certain, and that it will be a triumphal and glorious event, at least for Christians. However, for unbelievers, His return will bring rejection and judgment.

C. John 14:1–3. The night before Jesus was crucified, He told His disciples that He would soon be betrayed and leave them (13:21, 33, 36–38). Because His comments deeply distressed them, He spoke these comforting words:

> "Let not your heart be troubled; believe in God, believe also in Me. In My Father's house are many dwelling places; if it were not so, I would have told you; for I go to prepare a place for you. And if I go and prepare a place for you, I will come again, and receive you to Myself; that where I am, there you may be also." (14:1–3)

Jesus reassured them with two promises. First, He said He was going away to prepare a heavenly home for them—one where they could dwell forever in peace. Second, He guaranteed He would return personally to take them to their new home. And this applies to all believers. One day, the Lord will come back to move His children from earth to heaven, from the corruptible to the incorruptible, from a life of pain to one of everlasting bliss. That's something for us who are Christians to look forward to!

D. Acts 1:6–11. Three days after Jesus' crucifixion, He rose from the dead, conquering death forever. Then, over a forty-day period, He "presented Himself alive [to the disciples] . . . by many convincing proofs" (v. 3). At the end of this time, the disciples asked Him again about His return (v. 6). Christ's answer was simple and specific: " 'It is not for you to know times or epochs which the Father has fixed by His own authority; but you shall receive power when the Holy Spirit has come upon you; and you shall be My witnesses both in Jerusalem, and in all Judea and Samaria, and even to the remotest part of the earth' " (vv. 7–8). With these words still fresh in their minds, the disciples watched Jesus ascend into heaven (vv. 9–10a). Suddenly, two angels appeared and spoke to the them: " 'Men of Galilee, why do you stand looking into the sky? This Jesus, who has been taken up from you into heaven, will come in just the same way as you have watched Him go into heaven' " (v. 11). The angels repeated Jesus' message: Christ is coming again, but until He returns, His followers are to stop staring into the sky and start living as responsible Christians in a needy world. That's our task—nothing less.

IV. Scriptures That Describe Our Destiny

As we have already seen, our ultimate future is wrapped up with the return of Jesus Christ. Let's delve into this fact a bit more by focusing on two key passages.

A. First Corinthians 15:50–58. In these verses Paul explains what was previously shrouded in mystery. He says that although we are all in the process of dying, at some future time we will be changed "in a moment, in the twinkling of an eye" (v. 52). Our perishable bodies will become imperishable; our mortality will be robed in immortality (vv. 52b–54). This miraculous change will occur when Jesus returns, and it will happen to Christians both alive and dead. From that incredible moment on, Christians will live and rule with their Savior forever, completely free from and victorious over sin and its devastating effects (vv. 54b–57). "Therefore," Paul adds, "be steadfast, immovable, always abounding in the work of the Lord, knowing that your toil is not in vain in the Lord" (v. 58).

B. First Thessalonians 4:13–18. Here Paul further details what will occur when Christ returns. We can gather what he says under five directives.

1. **We are to be informed** (v. 13a). Ignorance is not bliss. We need to know, at least in broad brush strokes, what God has planned for the future so that we can live more confidently in the present.

2. **We are not to grieve like those without hope** (v. 13b). When a believer we love dies, it's only natural that we express our loss in tears. However, if we know that death does not close the book on one's life, our sorrow will be accompanied by the expectation of a better existence for our Christian friend or believing loved one. How different is the pain of loss for those who view death as the end of life! They have nothing to give them hope or comfort.

3. **We are to face death without fear** (v. 14). Since Jesus has overcome death by rising from the grave, we who have trusted in Him can also expect to experience victory over death. Therefore, we have nothing to fear.

4. **We are to know the order of events** (vv. 15–17). Paul cites four future happenings for us to remember. First, "the Lord

Himself will descend from heaven." Second, "the dead in Christ shall rise first." Third, "we who are alive and remain shall be caught up together with them." Finally, all of us will rise up to "the clouds to meet the Lord in the air, and thus we shall always be with the Lord." Many Christians believe that these events describe the Rapture of the Church. After this transition into heaven, a seven-year period of intense divine judgment will occur on earth. In biblical history, this time span is known as the Great Tribulation. It will end with Christ coming back to the earth to defeat His remaining enemies, fulfill His promises to the nation of Israel, and establish a thousand-year reign of world peace and prosperity.[2]

5. We are to comfort one another with this knowledge (v. 18). One day, we who are Christians will be reunited with all our believing family members, friends, and fellow saints. We will finally see and live forever with all those we miss now. That's something in which we can find encouragement and strength.

V. Actions That Reveal Our Readiness

How can we be prepared for Christ's imminent return? There are at least three ways we can show our readiness.

A. Walking by faith. Though we do not know *when* He will come again, we know that He *will,* and we should live responsibly in light of His return.

B. Living in peace. Present-day struggles need not overburden us. We can find rest in the fact that someday all things will be made right.

C. Relying on hope. Christ is our hope—our only hope. Because He lives and is coming again, we can live with the assurance that the final chapter of our lives is not death but everlasting life with Him. Do *you* have hope? Is your hope in the only person who can give it? If not, bring it into your life by trusting in Jesus Christ today.

Continued on next page

2. This understanding of the flow of end-time events is known as pretribulational millennialism. Not all Christians share this viewpoint. Two books that explain the various Christian perspectives on the future are *The Rapture: Pre-, Mid-, or Post-Tribulational?* by Richard R. Reiter et al. (Grand Rapids, Mich.: Academie Books, Zondervan Publishing House, 1984), and *The Meaning of the Millennium: Four Views,* ed. Robert G. Clouse (Downers Grove, Ill.: InterVarsity Press, 1977).

⚡ Living Insights

Two passages that help us understand the future are 1 Corinthians 15:50–58 and 1 Thessalonians 4:13–18. Let's see what each passage has to say about we who are Christians.

● As you read each passage, focus on two types of statements: those describing what will happen to us when Christ returns and those describing what we should do while we wait. Did you catch the difference? One section of each chart records things out of our control; the other section records things within our control.

1 Corinthians 15:50–58	
Verses	What Happens to Us?
Verses	What Should We Be Doing?

114

1 Thessalonians 4:13–18	
Verses	What Happens to Us?
Verses	What Should We Be Doing?

Continued on next page

🏛 *Living Insights*

His coming is sure ... are you? We concluded this lesson with three actions that reveal our readiness: walking by faith, living in peace, and relying on hope. Take a few minutes to answer the following questions on how you can make these activities a part of your life.

● How can you strengthen your faith?

_____

_____

_____

_____

_____

_____

_____

● How can you live peacefully in spite of the panic all around you?

_____

_____

_____

_____

_____

_____

_____

● In whom or in what are you placing your hope?

_____

_____

_____

_____

_____

_____

- How are faith, peace, and hope interrelated in your life?

_____

_____

_____

_____

_____

_____

_____

- What changes will be necessary for you to be ready for His coming?

_____

_____

_____

_____

_____

_____

_____

Until He Returns . . . What?

Selected Scripture

Christ is coming again—there's no doubt about it! But *when?* In the early 1840s, a preacher named William Miller calculated that Jesus would come around October 22, 1844. Believing his prediction, many of Miller's followers either sold or gave away their belongings. Needless to say, when the expected day came and Christ didn't appear, Miller and his movement lost face and credibility.[1] Although they were right to anticipate Jesus' return, they were wrong to set a date and to live irresponsibly while waiting. How *should* we conduct our lives as we anticipate Christ's return? Does God give us any counsel on this matter? He certainly does. Let's look into what He says.

I. Of These Things We Are Sure

Although no human being knows specifically when Christ's return will take place (Matt. 24:36, 42; Acts 1:6–7), we do know at least two things about it. First, we know Jesus' return is certain because He Himself said that it was (Matt. 25:31, Mark 8:38). Second, we understand that nothing stands in the way of His arrival. There is no event that must occur before Jesus comes back to resurrect and gather Christians to Himself. He could return on any day, at any moment (Matt. 24:42–44, James 5:7–9, Rev. 22:20).[2]

II. But in the Meantime . . .

Although Jesus could return today, He may not come for many years. What should we do while we are waiting? Four words sum up God's "marching orders" for us: *occupy, purify, watch,* and *worship.* Let's explore these biblical instructions.

   A. Occupy. In Luke 19:11–24, Jesus tells a parable that teaches us one thing we should do until He returns. It's a story about a nobleman who is planning to leave his estate for a while. Before leaving, he gives ten of his slaves one mina each—equivalent to approximately a hundred days' wages—and tells them to do business with it until his return. The nobleman didn't want his workers to sit back and await his arrival; instead, he wanted them to wisely invest the money he had entrusted to them. When the nobleman comes home, he asks those ten slaves to account for what they have done with his money. The first slave reports

1. See *Living in the Shadow of the Second Coming: American Premillennialism 1875–1982,* enlarged ed., by Timothy P. Weber (Grand Rapids, Mich.: Academie Books, Zondervan Publishing House, 1983), pp. 15–16.

2. For a more thorough treatment on the imminence of Christ's return, see "The Imminent Return of Jesus Christ," by Robert G. Gromacki, in *Grace Journal* (Fall 1965), pp. 11–23, and *The Rapture Question,* rev. ed., by John F. Walvoord (Grand Rapids, Mich.: Academie Books, Zondervan Publishing House, 1979), chap. 6.

that he has increased his mina tenfold. The second slave has also done well, multiplying his mina fivefold. Pleased with their productive diligence, the nobleman rewards these two slaves with an increase in authority and responsibility. However, when another slave says that he has held on to his mina, simply putting it away in a safe place, the nobleman angrily rebukes him and gives his money to the slave who had multiplied his mina tenfold.

Personal Application

Like the nobleman, Jesus wants us as His servants to get on with the business of living while He is away. This task involves realistic thinking, wise planning, diligent working, careful investing, and humble serving. We are to occupy His estate by maintaining and developing it until He returns. And for our labor, we will one day receive a generous reward (1 Cor. 3:10–14, 9:24–27; 2 Cor. 5:10).[3] However, we cannot do God's work His way if our lives are marked by indifference, laziness, or irresponsibility (2 Thess. 3:6–14). Are you living as a faithful servant of the King?

B. Purify. We are instructed to live godly lives in the present as we wait for Christ's future return. Notice how the Apostle Paul presents this idea in his letter to Titus:

> For the grace of God has appeared, bringing salvation to all men, instructing us to deny ungodliness and worldly desires and to live sensibly, righteously and godly in the present age, looking for the blessed hope and the appearing of the glory of our great God and Savior, Christ Jesus; who gave Himself for us, that He might redeem us from every lawless deed and purify for Himself a people for His own possession, zealous for good deeds. (Titus 2:11–14)

There is nothing like the anticipation of Jesus' return to motivate us to strive for integrity, moral purity, and spiritual vitality in our daily lives. In contrast, ponder the sorrow you would feel for presenting to Him a life of spiritual mediocrity.

Personal Application

How can our lives be characterized by holiness? First, we need to place as much emphasis on godly living as we do

---

3. A discussion on the rewards available to us is provided in the study guide *Improving Your Serve: The Art of Unselfish Living,* rev. ed., ed. Bill Watkins, from the Bible-teaching ministry of Charles R. Swindoll (Fullerton, Calif.: Insight for Living, 1986), pp. 76–79.

on the Lord's return. When a ministry teaches one area to the neglect of the other, it's a sure sign of imbalance at best and heresy at worst. Second, we need to live with short accounts. We dare not allow unconfessed sin to remain in our lives or neglect to attempt to right our wrongs. We must seek to keep a clear conscience, forgiving our offenders and making every effort to be reconciled to those we have offended (Matt. 5:23–24, 18:21–35). Are you letting God's power help you live a pure life?

C. Watch. Because Christ's return is imminent, we need to be alert. Jesus made this crystal clear:

> "Take heed, keep on the alert; for you do not know when the appointed time is. It is like a man, away on a journey, who upon leaving his house and putting his slaves in charge, assigning to each one his task, also commanded the doorkeeper to stay on the alert. Therefore, be on the alert—for you do not know when the master of the house is coming, whether in the evening, at midnight, at cockcrowing, or in the morning—lest he come suddenly and find you asleep. And what I say to you I say to all, 'Be on the alert!'" (Mark 13:33–37)

Those who keep a watchful eye for Jesus' return will be awarded "the crown of righteousness" by the Lord Himself (2 Tim. 4:8).

Personal Application

A practical way to maintain your vigilance is to remember each morning that this may be the day Christ comes back. You may even want to place a visual reminder—such as a picture or Bible verse—where you will see it often during the day. This may help you remember to be preparing yourself to meet the Lord face-to-face (Luke 12:35–40, 1 John 3:2). Do you daily anticipate His return?

D. Worship. Among the many acts of Christian worship is the memorial meal called communion, or the Lord's Supper—the meal believers are to celebrate together until Jesus comes again (1 Cor. 11:26). Every time we drink from the cup and eat of the bread, we should remind ourselves not only of Christ's death but also of His return.

> *Personal Application*
>
> Whenever we enjoy communion, let's use it as a time to look forward to Christ's coming as well as an opportunity to remember His substitutionary death. After all, each memorial meal we experience may be our last on earth. Do you think about Christ's return when you worship Him through the Lord's Supper?

III. How to Stay Alert and Ready

God's counsel to us can be summed up with three reminders.

A. Remember that Jesus promised He would return someday. Think of His coming when you read the newspaper, watch television news, or experience personal tragedies. Reminding yourself of the Lord's future return will help you through life's present struggles.

B. Realize that Jesus could return today. In any year, on any day, at any moment, you may hear Him call your name and see Him greet you with open arms. Prepare yourself daily for this event, for you do not know when it will happen.

C. Apply our marching orders: occupy, purify, watch, and worship. If you're regularly engaged in these activities, you won't have to *get* ready for Christ's coming—you'll *be* ready.

Living Insights

Study One

What does the Bible teach about how we should live until Jesus returns? As we learned in this lesson, the New Testament offers at least four specific instructions. Were you aware of all four or did a couple of these catch you by surprise?

- *Occupy, purify, watch, worship*—these four key words summarize much of what we're to do while waiting for Christ's coming. Review this lesson and pinpoint one area in which you're doing a good job. Next, determine which of the four areas you'd consider to be your weakest and do some more study on that subject. Reread the biblical texts that accompany the point in the lesson. Look for key words, principles, correlations, applications—all that you are able to glean on the topic. Perhaps you can broaden your search to include other passages of your own finding.

Continued on next page

Occupy: Luke 19:11–24; 1 Cor. 3:10–14, 9:24–27; 2 Cor. 5:10; 2 Thess. 3:6–14.

Purify: Matt. 5:23–24, 18:21–25; Titus 2:11–14.

Watch: Mark 13:33–37, Luke 12:35–40, 2 Tim. 4:8, 1 John 3:2.

Worship: 1 Cor. 11:26.

My Weakest Area: _____
Discoveries

 Living Insights

Study Two ▬▬▬▬▬▬▬▬▬▬▬▬▬▬▬▬▬▬▬▬▬▬▬▬▬▬▬▬

Christ's promised return gives us hope and anticipation. Yet, if you knew He was coming today, your life would probably change radically. What changes could you begin making now? Use the following questions to guide your thinking.

If Christ Came Today . . .

- Which of your present activities would bring great glory to God?

_____

_____

- Would you regret any of your current behavior or associations?

_____

_____

_____

_____

- What would He say about how you've handled your finances?

_____

_____

_____

_____

- What things would you wish you had done?

_____

_____

_____

_____

- What's keeping you from doing them?

_____

_____

_____

_____

Visiting the *Real* Twilight Zone

Selected Scripture

Eerie music and the chilling voice of Rod Serling have long transported television audiences from the dimension of the ordinary and mundane to that of the extraordinary and bizarre . . . "the twilight zone." The stories are fictional, but they contain an element of reality. There is another dimension to life we all must face. Beyond our earthly lives lies our ultimate destiny— the *real* twilight zone. And the only way to get there is through the portal of death. Join us now on a journey through the pages of Scripture to see what awaits us at death and beyond. The view on this trip will be unpleasant at times, but it will help us appreciate the eternal significance of the choice we make now—while we're alive.

I. Death: Inevitability and Effect

If Christ tarries, all of us are going to die. Our appointment with death cannot be canceled—the Scriptures make that abundantly plain. Consider just a sampling of its relevant passages:[1]

> "By the sweat of your brow you will eat your food until you return to the ground, since from it you were taken; for dust you are and to dust you will return." (Gen. 3:19)

> What man can live and not see death, or save himself from the power of the grave? (Ps. 89:48)

> Sin entered the world through one man, and death through sin, and in this way death came to all men, because all sinned. (Rom. 5:12)

> It is appointed for men to die once and after this comes judgment. (Heb. 9:27)

Some of us will die quickly and suddenly; others of us will suffer a slow, predictable death. We may not know in advance how or when death will happen, but we can be sure that it will come.

II. Resurrection: Promises and Procedure

What happens when we die? Do we cease to exist, or do we enter a different life beyond our earthly dimension? The Bible answers these questions, exposing the separate paths that await believers and unbelievers beyond the grave.

A. For Christians. If you believe in Jesus Christ, your material body—the "outer man" (2 Cor. 4:16) or "earthly tent" (5:1)—will continue to decay before and after death. At the same time, your

---

1. Except for Hebrews 9:27, the references in section I are from the New International Version.

immaterial soul and spirit[2]—occasionally referred to in Scripture as the "inner man" (4:16)—will continue to be restored into the image of Christ until death ushers them to a state of complete renewal (compare Col. 3:10–11). Death occurs when your soul and spirit separate from your body. The "inner you" will be immediately ushered into the presence of the Lord (2 Cor. 5:8), while the physical aspect of your being—your body—will decompose. During this entire process, you'll remain alert and conscious. And once you have left your body behind, you'll feel no pain, only joy and peace as you come before your loving Savior. Eventually, however, you will go through another change. When Jesus returns to gather to Himself Christians who are still alive, He will also resurrect the bodies of those Christians who have died (1 Thess. 4:14–17). In an instant, your spirit and soul will be reunited with your body. You will quickly find that your body is not as it was—corruptible and mortal, with sin flowing through its veins. It will be glorified—incorruptible, immortal, pregnant with the life-giving vitality you inherited by faith in Christ the Lord (1 Cor. 15:51–57). The resurrection of your body, its glorification, and the reunion of it to your soul and spirit will mark the completion of your restoration into Christ's image. For eternity, you will be as God the Father originally designed you to be— a perfect representation and representative of the Son of God (Rom. 8:29–30). You will live forever with the Lord and fellow saints in absolute bliss!

B. For non-Christians. If you are not a follower of Jesus Christ, your experience of physical death will be the same as the Christian's. With your last breath, your soul and spirit will separate from your body. However, you will not then go to be with the Lord in Paradise (Luke 23:43). You will leave your decaying body behind and enter a place of torment called Hades or hell (16:22–23). The degree of psychological and spiritual pain you will encounter there will make any suffering you endured on earth seem trivial. Then, when the curtains of history are about to draw to a close, your body will be resurrected and reunited to your soul and spirit. But nowhere does the Bible teach that your body will arise in a glorified state. Instead, you will stand before God, in a body

---

2. Some Christians do not believe that the soul and spirit are distinct aspects of human nature. They think that the terms *soul* and *spirit* in Scripture describe the same thing—the immaterial aspect of man. Those who accept this position are called dichotomists, while those who think that man has three distinct aspects to his nature—body, soul, and spirit—are trichotomists. These two viewpoints are discussed in Henry C. Thiessen's *Lectures in Systematic Theology,* rev. ed. (Grand Rapids, Mich.: William B. Eerdmans Publishing Co., 1979), pp. 160–62, and in G. C. Berkouwer's *Man: The Image of God* (1962; reprint, Grand Rapids, Mich.: William B. Eerdmans Publishing Co., 1981), chap. 6.

still marked by death, with all the other people who died without trusting in the Lord. You will be judged by your works, which are insufficient to save you. And you will be cast, says Jesus, " 'into the eternal fire which has been prepared for the devil and his angels' " (Matt. 25:41; compare Rev. 20:10–15, 21:8). There you will experience the ultimate punishment as a focal point of God's wrath (Rev. 14:9–11). There you'll begin the ultimate death— everlasting separation "from the presence of the Lord and from the glory of His power" (2 Thess. 1:9). This awful picture is the one in which you will find yourself if you don't place your faith in Christ before you die.

III. Destiny: Hell or Heaven

When unbelievers begin to take seriously the Bible's teaching on heaven and hell, they frequently respond in one of two ways.

A. The "earn-your-way-out" response. Some try to compensate for their lack of faith in Christ by becoming more religious. Rather than believing in Jesus, they continue to trust in their ability to save themselves, thinking, If I go to church regularly, study the Bible, and live a better life, surely God will keep me from going to hell. What these people fail to understand or accept is that religious practices cannot save. The Pharisees and scribes were probably the most religious individuals in Jesus' day. And yet, because they tried to order their lives without Christ at the center, they received a stern and revealing rebuke from Him: " 'You serpents, you brood of vipers, how shall you escape the sentence of hell?' " (Matt. 23:33). Only perfect righteousness can secure us for heaven, and that is available only through Jesus Christ.

B. The "excuse-your-way-out" response. Other unbelievers try to excuse themselves from the judgment of hell with rationalization. They think, It's not my fault if my eyes lust, my hands commit wrongs, and my feet lead me into sin. After all, I'm only human, and part of being human is making mistakes. With the use of hyperbole, Jesus refuted this reasoning, indicating that sin must be dealt with seriously and severely if hell is to be avoided:

> "And if your hand causes you to stumble, cut it off; it is better for you to enter life crippled, than having your two hands, to go into hell, into the unquenchable fire.... And if your foot causes you to stumble, cut it off; it is better for you to enter life lame, than having your two feet, to be cast into hell.... And if your eye causes you to stumble, cast it out; it is better for you to enter the kingdom of God with one eye, than having two eyes, to be cast into hell." (Mark 9:43–47)

IV. Preparation: Response and Result

Everyone must face two facts about life after death. First, the only time to prepare for then is *now.* Second, there is no chance to change after death. Remember Hebrews 9:27, which states, "It is appointed for men to die *once* and after this comes *judgment*" (emphasis added). After death, no one gets a second chance. Whatever we decide about our relationship to Christ in this life will be carried out in the next life, forever. We all will live eternally, but we won't all live eternally in the same place. Where we want to spend forever is up to each one of us. Which do you choose?

Continued on next page

Living Insights

Study One

The study of death is both morbid and intriguing. With the further assistance of God's Word, we can gain an even greater understanding of this topic.

- Earlier in this study guide we acquainted you with the art of paraphrasing. To refresh your memory, paraphrasing is putting the words of Scripture into your own words. Using the space provided, paraphrase the following three New Testament passages. These texts are crucial to understanding the *real* twilight zone!

2 Corinthians 5:1–8

_____

_____

_____

_____

_____

_____

_____

_____

_____

_____

_____

_____

_____

Matthew 25:31–34, 41

_____

_____

_____

_____

_____

_____

_____

_____

1 John 5:10–13

_____

_____

_____

_____

_____

_____

_____

_____

_____

_____

_____

_____

Continued on next page

For Christians, the most exciting experience of life is yet to come. Have you looked at heaven that way before?

● What are your thoughts about eternity—life after death? Jot them down in the space provided. Based on what you know from God's Word, what will heaven be like? If you are a Christian, what will heaven be like *for you?* Do you really believe it will be your most exciting experience? Contrast heaven with your life on earth, perhaps focusing on the hurts that will be healed and the trials that will cease.

Eternity . . . My Life after Death

An Interview with One from Beyond

Luke 16

"Death is the most universal and most democratic of all human functions. It strikes people at any time with little respect for age, class, creed, or color."[1] J. Kerby Anderson has hit the proverbial nail on the head. We all will experience death. But despite this inevitability, many Americans refused to discuss or even think about death until the 1970s. That decade saw a dramatic reversal within the United States. It changed from a death-denying culture to one seemingly obsessed with and insatiably curious about death and the afterlife. Unfortunately, this newfound interest has not led the public to a serious consideration of what the Bible says on this topic. Instead, the majority of people rely on subjective experiences, fanciful wishes, and incredible speculations to provide much of their information. Although we'll briefly mention some of this data below, we'll primarily focus on our only infallible source—God's Word—considering what it teaches about death and the afterlife.

I. What Broke the Silence Barrier?

America's renewed interest in death and the life beyond is a result of five contributing factors.[2] First, the medical profession has greatly heightened its research into thanatology, or the study of death—a change largely due to the work of thanatologist Elisabeth Kubler-Ross.[3] Second, many high schools, community colleges, universities, and medical schools now offer courses on death and dying. In some classes, students are required to visit mortuaries or conduct interviews with those who claim to have had an OBE—out-of-body experience. Third, with the increased number of films, television programs, and news articles on death-related issues, the media has done a great deal to make what was formerly unmentionable a frequent topic of discussion. Fourth, because technological advances now allow us to prolong life through artificial means, people are dealing with questions unheard of several years past—questions about the meaning, value, and end of life. And fifth, a growing pessimism regarding the ability of man to save himself from ecological or nuclear disaster has led many individuals to consider the evidence for an afterlife.

---

1. J. Kerby Anderson, *Life, Death and Beyond* (Grand Rapids, Mich.: Zondervan Publishing House, 1980), p. 9.

2. See Anderson, *Life, Death and Beyond*, pp. 12–14.

3. Two of the most influential books by Elisabeth Kubler-Ross are *On Death and Dying* (New York, N.Y.: Macmillan Publishing Co., 1969), and *Questions and Answers on Death and Dying* (New York, N.Y.: Macmillan Publishing Co., 1974).

II. Common Death-and-Dying Experiences

Much of the current attention being paid to thanatology surrounds out-of-body experiences, which usually occur during close calls with death, while dying, or after one appears to be dead. Although OBEs vary greatly, there are some events in these experiences that seem to crop up often.[4] For example, many people have said that during their OBE they found themselves in peaceful surroundings, saw flashbacks of major happenings in their lives, and viewed their physical bodies from a distance. Some individuals have reported seeing departed friends and relatives, while others claim to have passed through a tunnel where they were met by a being of light. One of the most common and intriguing OBE events is that of remaining connected to one's physical body while floating above it. Numerous people have described a silver cord attaching their physical and spiritual bodies. These individuals have almost all believed that this cord is the final link between life and death. Once it breaks, the spiritual permanently departs from the physical, resulting in death to the material body. A passage in Ecclesiastes 12 appears to confirm their belief: "Remember [your Creator] before the silver cord is broken and the golden bowl is crushed . . . ; then the dust will return to the earth as it was, and the spirit will return to God who gave it" (vv. 6–7). While the Bible does not tell us whether every event described by OBE participants is true, it does unveil what God wants believers and unbelievers to know about death and the life beyond.

III. Biblical Hope for Christians to Claim

As we saw in the last lesson, Christians have been assured by the Lord that, at the moment of death, they will be immediately transported into His presence in heaven, although their bodies will continue to decay on earth. Then, when Jesus returns to remove all Christians from the earth, the bodies of deceased believers will be resurrected from their graves, renewed into the image of Christ, and reunited to the souls and spirits that once animated them. In this state of perfection, Christians will be like Christ in His resurrected condition. They will be incorruptible, immortal, and completely free from sin and its effects (1 Cor. 15:51–57). Their bodies will be of imperishable flesh and bone (Luke 24:37–39), and they will be capable of moving from one time-space dimension to another at will (vv. 13–15, 30–31; John 20:19, 26). In this resurrected state, Christians will serve and enjoy their Savior forever (Matt. 25:19–23, 29; Rev. 21:2–4, 10–26, 22:1–5). Little wonder believers have no reason to fear death—for them, it is the gate to everlasting peace and happiness (2 Cor. 5:8, Phil. 1:21–23).

---

4. See Anderson, *Life, Death and Beyond*, chaps. 5–7.

IV. Ultimate Realities for Non-Christians to Face

The destiny non-Christians face is very different from what Christians can anticipate. This truth is graphically presented by Jesus in Luke 16, where we are made privy to an interview, if you will, with one from beyond.

A. Life before death. Jesus turns our attention to two people—an unnamed rich man and a poor beggar named Lazarus. The wealthy man " 'habitually dressed in purple and fine linen, gaily living in splendor every day' " (v. 19). In contrast, Lazarus " 'was laid at [the rich man's] gate, covered with sores, and longing to be fed with the crumbs which were falling from the rich man's table' " (vv. 20–21). The beggar was a believer; the wealthy man, an unbeliever.

B. Life after death. Eventually, the two men died. Lazarus " 'was carried away by the angels to Abraham's bosom' " (v. 22)—evidently a place of paradise for those who were saved under the Old Testament economy.[5] The rich man, on the other hand, found himself in Hades (v. 23a), the abode of all dead unbelievers until the Great White Throne judgment following the millennial reign of Christ (Rev. 20:7, 11–15). As the account unfolds, we discover that the man who once lived in great luxury and comfort was now suffering extreme agony (Luke 16:23a). Seeing Lazarus in peaceful surroundings, the former rich man cried out to Abraham, who was comforting the onetime beggar: " ' "Father Abraham, have mercy on me, and send Lazarus, that he may dip the tip of his finger in water and cool off my tongue; for I am in agony in this flame" ' " (v. 24). Abraham, however, denied his request, reminding him that he had selfishly enjoyed his wealth on earth while Lazarus had lived in abject poverty. Now the tables were turned: the former beggar was receiving the riches of faith, and the once-wealthy man was experiencing the privations of unbelief (v. 25). Moreover, the post-death situations of the two men were permanently fixed by a great chasm that made it impossible for those on either side of it to cross over (v. 26). Once the man in Hades realized this, he pleaded with Abraham to send Lazarus back to life on earth. He thought that if someone were to rise from the dead and warn his five brothers about what awaits unbelievers in the afterlife, they would surely repent and be spared everlasting torment (vv. 27–28, 30). Once again, Abraham rejected his request, telling the man that his brothers had the Scriptures, which were sufficient to reveal the way to everlasting life with God. If his relatives chose to reject the testimony of

---

5. John A. Martin, "Luke," in *The Bible Knowledge Commentary: New Testament Edition*, ed. John F. Walvoord and Roy B. Zuck (Wheaton, Ill.: Victor Books, 1983), p. 247.

God's Word, they would certainly refuse to believe the witness of a resurrected saint (vv. 29, 31).

C. Some conclusions on the afterlife. This account reveals several significant truths about life beyond the grave. First, the deceased are conscious and able to feel, reason, remember, hear, and talk. Second, the saved enjoy everlasting bliss; the lost suffer unending anguish. Third, death eternally finalizes the choice a person makes about trusting in God while alive. No one gets a second chance. Fourth, unbelievers awaiting the final judgment have a belated evangelistic zeal for their unsaved loved ones on earth. How much more so should we who are saved and still have the opportunity to share the gospel! And fifth, the most effective witnessing tool is the Bible—God's Word to man. Its impact on lives is more profound than even the testimony of one who rises from the dead (compare John 11:43–57, 12:9–11). Realizing this, we ought to use it far more than many of us do when we present the good news about Christ.

V. Major Questions Worth Answering

Discussions of death and the afterlife naturally raise some questions. Let's consider the five that come up most frequently.

A. How can a loving God send people to hell? This question seems to imply that God is cruel, delighting in unfairly sentencing people to eternal damnation. Scripture does not paint this portrait of God. Rather, He is presented as the sovereign, just, compassionate Lord of the universe (Deut. 32:4; Pss. 22:28, 145:8–9). He is the giver and sustainer of life (Gen. 1, John 1:1–3, Acts 17:25, Col. 1:16–17); consequently, only He has the right and the authority to establish the ground rules for salvation—namely, that faith in Christ alone leads to everlasting life (John 14:6, Acts 4:10–12). Those who freely choose to die in a state of unbelief receive the rightful consequences of their decision—separation from God forever. As C. S. Lewis so aptly states it:

> "There are only two kinds of people in the end: those who say to God, 'Thy will be done,' and those to whom God says, in the end, 'Thy will be done.' All that are in Hell, choose it. Without that self-choice there could be no Hell. No soul that seriously and constantly desires joy will ever miss it. Those who seek find. To those who knock it is opened."[6]

And as the Apostle Peter declares, God is patiently waiting for unbelievers to knock on the door leading to salvation, because He does "not [wish] for any to perish but for all to come to repentance" (2 Pet. 3:9).

6. C. S. Lewis, *The Great Divorce* (New York, N.Y.: Macmillan Publishing Co., 1946), pp. 72–73.

B. What about those who have never heard about Christ yet sincerely follow their own religious beliefs? Are they destined for hell? We know from Scripture that Christ is the personal revealer of the Godhead (John 1:18, 6:45–46) and the only divinely approved Savior (3:16–17, 5:19–40, 6:38–40; Heb. 1:1–4, 10:10–14). He has said, " 'I am *the* way, and *the* truth, and *the* life; *no one* comes to the Father, *but through Me.*' " (John 14:6, emphasis added). Therefore, anyone who refuses to accept Him as Savior is headed for everlasting death. We should understand, however, that the Lord uses a multitude of means to get our attention. Nature, the Bible, the Holy Spirit, our consciences, friends, family, preachers, evangelists, circumstances, books, pamphlets, cassettes, and films are just a few of the avenues God uses to reveal Himself and His Messiah to us. Everyone has an adequate witness to the way of salvation; as a result, everyone who rejects it is without an excuse (Rom. 1:18–23, 2:14–16, 10:9–21). However, all who die in unbelief will not receive punishment to the same degree. Those who reject Christ with little knowledge of Him will not be punished as severely as those who refuse to believe in Him although they have had abundant exposure to His claims (Matt. 11:20–24, Luke 12:47–48). Certainly, all unbelievers will end up in hell if they don't repent. However, they will not all suffer equally.

C. What about deathbed repentance? Can people be saved if they trust in Christ so close to death? Yes—if we sincerely put our faith in Jesus, we inherit everlasting life regardless of our proximity to death. This is verified by the account of the thief who was promised life in Paradise while he was dying on a cross next to Jesus (Luke 23:39–43).

D. What about children who die before they gain the ability to comprehend spiritual matters? The answer to this is embedded in 2 Samuel 12:23, where David makes the following comment concerning his infant son who has just died: " 'I shall go to him, but he will not return to me.' " David knew that he would see his child again when, following death, he entered into God's presence. We also know that God's heart is tender toward little children. Thus, we can be assured of the destiny of our little ones who die before they are capable of accepting Christ.[7]

E. Is the theory of reincarnation true? Not at all! In the passage just cited, we saw that David understood that his deceased child would not come back to him from the grave. Job

---

7. A thorough treatment of this issue is provided by Robert P. Lightner in his book *Heaven for Those Who Can't Believe* (Schaumburg, Ill.: Regular Baptist Press, 1977).

also realized that once someone was gone, that person was gone for good (Job 7:8–10). The writer of Hebrews crystallized the teaching of Scripture in one statement: "It is appointed [by God] for men to die *once* and after this comes judgment" (Heb. 9:27, emphasis added). One day, all the dead will be resurrected to a life of everlasting happiness or everlasting anguish. At no time, however, will anyone be reincarnated to live again, die again, live again, die again, and so on.[8] Death seals our decisions for eternity (Luke 16:26–31).

VI. Where Are *You* Going to Spend Eternity?

If you deny the inevitability of death, you are lying to yourself. However, to deny the Savior is far more tragic; you might as well sentence yourself to death for now and always. Are you still on death row, refusing to accept Christ's full and eternal pardon? If so, remember the rich man Jesus talked about. When he was alive, he didn't believe in Christ either. Now he knows better . . . but it's too late.

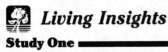 *Living Insights*

Study One ▬▬▬▬▬▬▬▬▬▬▬▬▬▬▬▬▬▬▬▬▬▬▬▬

Those who ignore the Word of God in life will not be ignored by the God of the Word in eternity. That sentence summarizes the account of the rich man and Lazarus in Luke 16:19–31. This account demands our attention. Let's give it some further study.

- The story of the rich man and Lazarus is familiar to many of us. Yet the urgency of the message may need to be communicated afresh in our lives. One way to see the story in a new way is to reread it in another version of the Scriptures. Check out The Living Bible or the paraphrase of the New Testament by J. B. Phillips. You should experience more of the emotion of the story as a result of interacting with these different editions.

8. A complete and up-to-date evaluation of reincarnation is given by Norman L. Geisler and J. Yutaka Amano in their book *The Reincarnation Sensation* (Wheaton, Ill.: Tyndale House, 1986).

Living Insights

Our look at the doctrine of resurrection has been quite heavy. Let's pause a few minutes to reflect and catch our breath.

- Why not leave this Living Insights study wide open? You can spend your time in a variety of ways. Perhaps you could use it to pray, talking to God about what you've learned, or to review some of the doctrinal teaching that has been new to you, or to discuss these issues with a close friend or family member. Choose one of these suggestions or create your own. The key is to engage in an activity that will help you apply what you're learning.

God's Body-building Program

Matthew 16:16–18, Acts, 1 Corinthians

Imagine the Christian doctrines we have been surveying depicted by paintings in an art gallery. Entering the gallery, we find a hallway lined with paintings presenting the Bible as God's guidebook for our lives. Stepping into a majestic, dome-shaped room, we stand in awe of pieces of art that symbolize God's radiant nature and infinite love. In hallway after hallway, room after room, we discover paintings of God's redemptive work throughout human history.

Something, however, seems to be missing. We ask the tour guide if there is a room we have not seen yet—one that captures God's program for man from Christ's ascension to His return. "I see," says the guide, "you want me to show you what the Lord kept hidden until the day of Pentecost. Follow me." Walking past rooms marked The Creation, The Fall, The Flood, The Mosaic Law, and The First Coming of the Messiah, we finally enter a chamber filled with portraits of saints from the age of the apostles down through the twentieth century. A sign is nailed to a cross above the doorway. It reads The Church: God's Body-building Program. The paintings reveal that the Lord is presently using those He saves through His Son, Jesus Christ, to construct His worldwide Church. Let's spend some additional time in this room so that we can learn more about God's contemporary miracle—the Church.

I. A Brief Historical Survey

This room displays a panoramic portrayal of the history of the Church. Let's look more closely at the representations of the major periods.

A. The Apostolic Age. The period of the Church began when the Holy Spirit came upon the apostles in a mighty way on the day of Pentecost (Acts 2). This incredible event occurred just days after the apostles saw Jesus ascend into heaven (1:9–11). The first several years of the Church were marked by rapid growth and purifying persecution. By the end of the first century A.D., the Roman Empire had been turned upside down with the Christian message of the gospel.

B. The age of the church fathers. This period of church history encompasses the second, third, and fourth centuries. During this time the Church continued to grow, challenging the heathen of her day with the claims and power of Christ. This was also a period in which believers began a united effort to clarify and systematize the Bible's teaching about the nature and work of Jesus Christ. Two men who were of great help in this task were Athanasius (A.D. 293–373) and Augustine (340–397). By the year 313, "Christianity [had become] an officially recognized religion in the Roman Empire. Moreover, by the end of the century the Roman rulers . . . decreed that Christianity was the sole official religion of the empire."[1]

C. The Middle Ages. The exaltation of Christianity to the official religion of Rome eventually led to the Church's corruption. Ecclesiastical leaders became more concerned about gaining power over civil governments than about proclaiming the gospel and equipping the saints for ministry. The biggest losers in the clergy's pursuit of political domination were the Church's lay-people. Due to the lack of biblical instruction, they became scripturally ignorant and spiritually ineffective. But all was not bleak. Some bright, well-trained believers contributed considerably to the growth of the Church, two of whom were Anselm (1033–1109) and Thomas Aquinas (1225–1274).[2] However, generally speaking, the latter centuries of the Middle Ages cast a dark shadow over Europe, the Middle East, and northern Africa.

D. The Reformation. During the fourteenth, fifteenth, and sixteenth centuries, courageous individuals began taking a stand against corruption in the Church. Christians like John Wycliffe (1324–1384), John Huss (1369–1415), Martin Luther (1483–1546), and John Calvin (1509–1564) fought against spiritual lethargy and decadence, basing their denouncements on the superior authority of God's Word. Their zeal and vision spread like wildfire across the continents, challenging unbiblical doctrines and practices. Europe, England, and eventually America were ablaze with the spiritual revival started by these Protestants.

E. The twentieth-century Church. Believers today are, in most cases, benefactors of the protest movements that started during the Reformation. This is because the Reformation's key leaders rethought, restated, and reintroduced two of Christianity's major doctrines—*soteriology* (the doctrine of salvation) and *ecclesiology* (the doctrine of the Church). These two areas of theology go hand in hand, as we will shortly see.

II. Some Essentials about the Church

Unlike local churches, which can decline in membership, the universal Church is constantly growing due to the continual addition of new Christians. As the years pass by, some of the Church's members backslide or die, but they never lose their membership. God holds them securely in their faith-commitment to Him so that He

---

1. R. D. Linder, "Church and State," in *Evangelical Dictionary of Theology,* ed. Walter A. Elwell (Grand Rapids, Mich.: Baker Book House, 1984), p. 234.

2. An excellent Protestant assessment of the beliefs of Thomas Aquinas is given by Arvin Vos in his book *Aquinas, Calvin, and Contemporary Protestant Thought: A Critique of Protestant Views on the Thought of Thomas Aquinas,* foreword by Ralph McInerny (Washington, D.C.: Christian University Press, 1985).

can "make [them] stand in the presence of His glory blameless with great joy" (Jude 24; compare John 10:2–5, 27–30).

A. The Church predicted. The first mention of the Church falls from the lips of Jesus during His earthly ministry. Toward the end of a dialogue between Himself and His disciples, Jesus blesses Simon for identifying Him as " 'the Christ, the Son of the living God' " (Matt. 16:16–17). Then Christ calls Simon *Petros,* or Peter, which means "rock," and prophesies that " 'upon this rock [*petra,* or rocklike truth] I will build My church; and the gates of Hades shall not overpower it' " (v. 18). In other words, not Peter but his confession about Jesus' identity was the foundation on which Christ said He would build His Church.[3] Also, Jesus' words leave no doubt that the Church belongs to Him, and that He is her builder. Neither ministers nor laypeople have ultimate authority over His Body-building project. He alone is the head of the Church (Eph. 1:20–23, 5:23–24; Col. 1:16–18). And because He is the Lord of all, He can fulfill His promise that the forces of death and evil, try as they might, will never destroy or defeat the Church. The building of the Church will continue until the Lord has brought His project to completion.

B. The Church defined. The Greek word for "church" is *ekklēsia,* which is made up of a preposition and a verb that together mean "to call out from among." The Church, therefore, is comprised of those individuals who have been chosen by Christ for salvation. When they hear Him call, through whatever means He decides to use, they come willingly (John 10:1–4, 7–16). And they come from all backgrounds, all creeds, all nations, all languages, and all races. In brief, the Church is *the ever-enlarging body of born-again believers who comprise the universal Body of Christ over whom He reigns as Lord.* Becoming members of and servants in this worldwide body of Christians is the most life-changing and meaningful thing we can ever do. "When people begin to realize that Church [is] a passion for living with eternal dimensions, it revolutionizes their whole frame of reference. Their world suddenly enlarges from this tiny speck of time and circumstances to a worldwide, invincible project over which Christ serves as Lord."[4]

---

3. Louis A. Barbieri, Jr., adopts this interpretation in his commentary "Matthew," in *The Bible Knowledge Commentary: New Testament Edition* (Wheaton, Ill.: Victor Books, 1983), p. 57. Some other interpretations of this controversial passage are proposed and defended in *The Church in God's Program,* by Robert L. Saucy (Chicago, Ill.: Moody Press, 1972), pp. 62–64; *Difficult Passages in the Gospels,* by Robert H. Stein (Grand Rapids, Mich.: Baker Book House, 1984), pp. 86–88; and "Matthew," by D. A. Carson, in *The Expositor's Bible Commentary* (Grand Rapids, Mich.: Regency Reference Library, Zondervan Publishing House, 1984), vol. 8, pp. 366–69.

4. Charles R. Swindoll, *Growing Deep in the Christian Life* (Portland, Oreg.: Multnomah Press, 1986), p. 339.

III. Rapid Growth of the Early Church

Returning to the paintings of the Apostolic Age, we find ample evidence of the Church's tremendous development during her early years. For example, on the day the Church was born, three thousand people became members (Acts 2:41). They met regularly in different homes and involved themselves in the four essentials of spiritual growth: obedience to biblical instruction, development of Christian fellowship, participation in the ordinances (water baptism and communion), and devotion to prayer (vv. 42, 46–47a). As they committed themselves to the Lord, new members were added to their church rolls (v. 47, 5:14). Even many Jewish priests came to believe in Jesus as their Messiah (6:7). But all was not easy for these first Christians. The growth of the Church was accompanied by increased persecution. This, however, served to cleanse the Church and caused her to spill over the city limits of Jerusalem into " 'all Judea and Samaria, and even to the remotest part of the earth' " (1:8b; compare 8:1–8, 9:31, 11:19–26, 12:24, 16:5–12, 19:17–20, 28:30–31).

IV. Changes That Occur When We Believe

The Church grew as quickly as she did primarily because Christ had been welcomed into people's lives by faith. She continues to expand in the same way today. What happens when Christ enters our lives? The twofold answer will help us understand how we can be changed from pagans to saints so rapidly, completely, and irreversibly.

A. Something happens *within* us. When we place our trust in Jesus, we become new creatures (2 Cor. 5:17). Our self-centered orientation becomes a selfless one. We gain new motivations, new interests, new abilities, and new resources (Rom. 6:4, 12:1–21; 2 Cor. 5:14–15; Eph. 4:11–5:2, 6:10–18). We desire to spend time with God and glorify Him rather than rebel against Him and hide.

B. Something happens *to* us. Our act of faith in Christ also leads immediately to our adoption into God's forever family (Gal. 4:3–7). This means that we become brothers and sisters in Christ, joint heirs of the imperishable and abundant riches of our heavenly Father (Rom. 8:15–17, 1 Tim. 5:1–2).

V. Signs of Health and Illness in the Church

Although the universal Body of Christ is alive and growing, not all local expressions of His Body are spiritually healthy. We can determine the health of a congregation by looking for signs of vitality and by recognizing the diseases that often debilitate a local church, thereby hampering the effectiveness of the universal Church.

A. Vital signs of a healthy church. One telltale sign of a fit church is *the presence of unity and harmony* (1 Cor. 12:12; compare John 17:20–23, Eph. 4:1–6). Just as a healthy physical body is marked by the cooperative activity of its organs, so a spiritually fit congregation displays a oneness of purpose among its many members. Another sign of good health is *the absence of favoritism, status, and prejudice* (1 Cor. 12:13, Gal. 3:26–28). Believers in a healthy local assembly treat one another as equals, regardless of occupation, community standing, income, race, sex, or ecclesiastical position. A third earmark of spiritual vitality is *an emphasis on individual dignity and mutual variety* (1 Cor. 12:14–20). All Christians are treated with respect and encouraged to exercise their gifts to "the growth of the body for the building up of itself in love" (Eph. 4:16). *A de-emphasis on independence and self-sufficiency* is another indication of a healthful church (1 Cor. 12:21–25a). The Lone Ranger mentality is not promoted or accepted. Believers are urged to work together to carry out the ministry of the Church. Along with this sign is yet another one—*the support of others, whether they are hurting or being honored* (vv. 25b–26). Strong churches rush to the aid of Christians who have fallen on hard times, and they rejoice with believers who are reaping the rewards of their labors. One last mark of health is *the exaltation of Christ as the head and the supreme authority* (v. 27). Leaders and laypeople of dynamic congregations strive to place their lives and their ministries under the lordship of Jesus Christ.

B. Contagious diseases that cripple a church. Comparing a local congregation to the human body helps us imagine how sin can spread stifling infections throughout a body of believers. For instance, pride can swell the mind of a church, while indifference to wrongdoing can chill the heart of a congregation. Unapplied theology can clog an assembly's digestive system, causing it to become spiritually and ministerially ineffective. Eyes that feed on lust and greed, tongues that wag, and ears that soak up gossip can blind, divide, and poison a church and damage its witness to the community. The local church also suffers when it has knees that seldom bow to Christ's authority; imaginations that are closed to new ideas; emotions that are out of control or under rigid wraps; and rarely exercised muscles of the mind, finances, or faith. Unless churches submit to the health plan of their divine Physician, they will hurt not only themselves but the rest of the Body of Christ as well.

VI. Checking Your Health and Commitment to the Church

Now that we've examined the Church's health, from the day of its birth on through its growing-up years and into adulthood, let's redirect our attention. What about *your* spiritual health? Are you contributing to the Church's growth? Are you personally involved in

Bible study? Are you serving believers in a local church and spreading the gospel in your community? Are you in the habit of petitioning and praising God in prayer? Honestly, now, how would you answer these questions?

Living Insights

Study One

Christ's Body, the Church, is much like our human bodies—to a large degree, its health can be determined by monitoring its vital signs. Let's pursue this medical exam a little further.

- The following exercise lists the six vital signs of a healthy church. Since we uncovered all of these signs in 1 Corinthians, let's go on a little "Scripture search" to find out what else the Bible has to say about them. Using a concordance, find at least two other verses dealing with these signs. Under each heading, write the references; then jot down some of the principles you learn from these passages.

The Presence of Unity and Harmony

Passages   Principles

_____   _____

                           _____

_____   _____

                           _____

_____   _____

                           _____

The Absence of Favoritism, Status, and Prejudice

Passages   Principles

_____   _____

                           _____

_____   _____

                           _____

Continued on next page

143

_____ _____

                    _____

An Emphasis on Individual Dignity and Mutual Variety

Passages   Principles

_____ _____

                    _____

_____ _____

                    _____

_____ _____

A De-emphasis on Independence and Self-Sufficiency

Passages   Principles

_____ _____

                    _____

_____ _____

                    _____

_____ _____

Support of Others, whether They Are Hurting or Being Honored

Passages   Principles

_____ _____

                    _____

_____ _____

                    _____

_____ _____

                    _____

The Exaltation of Christ as Head and the Supreme Authority

Passages   Principles

_____   _____
                     _____

_____   _____
                     _____

_____   _____
                     _____

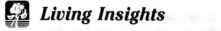 *Living Insights*

Let's take the analogy of the Body of Christ one step further—to a personal level. What part of the human body best describes *your* functions in the Body of Christ?

● In the space provided, put your thoughts on the following questions into words: What part of the body is most like you—a hand, a foot, an ear, a lung, an elbow? Why do you think so? How is your role important to the whole Body of Christ? When you've finished, perhaps it would be fun to compare answers with friends or family members who answered the same questions.

My Part in the Body of Christ

_____

_____

_____

_____

_____

_____

_____

_____

Three Cheers for the Church

Philippians 1

What a remarkable thing Christ is doing! Out of every continent, country, city, village, and tribe, He is recruiting undeserving individuals into service in His Body, the Church. As a result, pockets of people the world over gather to celebrate their faith. Music, messages, and love mingle to refresh sagging spirits, confront wrong, model truth, help the hurting, rescue the perishing, and care for the dying. During their times of corporate worship, they frequently observe two ancient ordinances unique to Christianity—the Lord's Supper and water baptism. How privileged we are to live in the period of history God has chosen to begin and build His Church! For the next few moments, let's lay any negative thoughts aside and zero in on what is good about the local church—the microcosm of the Church universal.

I. For a Few Minutes, Remember Some Churches

Many of us were fortunate to grow up in a local church. Despite any shortcomings it may have had, we likely have some very pleasant memories about that church. Let's take a walk down memory lane, allowing the letter of Philippians to act as our guide.

A. Days of childhood. As a child, you may have attended an urban church located in a busy section of town or a little country church nestled among some trees. Regardless of the church's location or size, chances are you feel the same way Paul did about the church in Philippi: "I thank my God in all my remembrance of you, always offering prayer with joy in my every prayer for you all, in view of your participation in the gospel from the first day until now" (Phil. 1:3–5). In the church of your youth, you probably received formal instruction on Christianity for the first time in your life. You listened to hymns, Bible stories, and sermons that you didn't fully understand at first but later began to appreciate. More importantly, you received in that church your initial impressions of the centrality of Christ and the difference He can make in a life. You got to know people who were committed to God regardless of the personal cost. You had a chance to laugh with them, weep with them, celebrate with them, and even encourage them. Are you beginning to remember?

B. Times of crisis. Of course, all your experiences were not filled with joy. As you grew older, periods of discouragement, failure, resentment, and maybe deep grief hung over your life. Perhaps you lost your mother, father, brother, sister, or mate. You may have left a doctor's office reeling from the news that you had a crippling, even life-endangering disease. Maybe your spouse divorced you, your teenager ran away, you were out of work for several months, or your home caught fire and burned to the ground. Who came to your aid, giving you a chance to share your feelings without fear of condemnation? Who reached out with financial help, the right counsel, and words of hope mixed with actions of love? Quite likely, it was people from your church. When the going got tough, they hung in there, perhaps when everyone else had given up hope (vv. 7–8, 4:10–18).

C. Moments of celebration. As the memories come alive, you may recall that you were married in a church by a pastor who had played a significant part in your spiritual growth. Maybe he later dedicated your children to the Lord. Who applauded your graduation from high school . . . college . . . seminary? Who rejoiced with you when your children accepted Christ and your teens recommitted themselves to the Lord? Who praised God with you when you landed that needed job, received that well-earned promotion, or finally moved into that first house? In all likelihood, it was your church family. They may have even encouraged you more than your natural family.

II. Why the Church Is So Significant

Returning to the present, let's look at three areas where the local church plays a crucial role. What we will discover has practical implications for our personal lives as well.

A. In the world. The Apostle Paul's ministry made the gospel of Christ "well-known throughout the whole [Roman] praetorian guard and to everyone else," and it gave "most of the brethren . . . far more courage to speak the word of God without fear" (Phil. 1:13–14). The local church reaps similar results today. Why? Because it is filled with believers who are beacons of light and preservers of life in a dark, dying world (compare Matt. 5:13–16). In fact, churches are often criticized by the public when they fail to take a clear stand on important moral issues. Even if unbelievers are confused about what merits the labels Wrong and Right, they still expect churches to be hard on sin. Are you uncompromising with sin? Do you stand up for what's right?

B. In the community. In Philippians 1:15–18, Paul says:

Some, to be sure, are preaching Christ even from envy and strife, but some also from good will; the latter do it out of love, knowing that I am appointed for the defense of the gospel; the former proclaim Christ out of selfish ambition, rather than from pure motives, thinking to cause me distress in my imprisonment. What then? Only that in every way, whether in pretense or in truth, Christ is proclaimed; and in this I rejoice, yes, and I will rejoice.

Paul is telling us that though churches may vary, they offer a singular message: we can be free from sin's penalty, power, and presence through Christ. From church to church, this message is conveyed by different methods, with different emphases, and for different reasons—none of which are more important than the message itself. This variety of ministries and approaches makes it possible for more people to be reached with the basic truths of Christianity than could ever be reached otherwise. That realization should prod us to encourage, not unduly criticize, the development and success of different churches and ministries. Are you attending a church that presents and exalts Christ? Do you rejoice when people find a fellowship that ministers to them, even if it is not your church?

C. For the Christian. The church is special to Christians because it is the only institution that exhorts them and helps them "conduct [themselves] in a manner worthy of the gospel of Christ" (v. 27a). In fact, there are at least four benefits that come from regularly attending a Christ-centered church: accountability, consistency, unity, and stability. Do these traits mark your life?

III. Two Ordinances Unique to the Church

Another special truth about the Church is that it alone has been given two sacraments by God. One is the Lord's Supper, also called communion, the Eucharist, or simply the Lord's table. It is a celebration of Christ's death and all it accomplished. The other ordinance is water baptism, which is a celebration of Christ's resurrection and its impact on a believer's life. Both of these sacraments are for Christians only, and both were established to remind believers of what Christ has done for them. Neither is a requirement for salvation, yet both are extremely significant in the Christian life. Let's consider each one in a little more depth.

A. The Lord's Supper. The elements of communion—some wine or juice and bread—are simple, but they have great significance. The bread stands for Christ's body, which was broken for us; the drink is a symbol of Christ's blood, which was shed for us (Matt. 26:26–28). Jesus commanded His people to keep on observing this memorial meal until He returns for them (1 Cor. 11:23–26). Participation in this rite is not optional. Every Christian should observe it regularly and take it seriously. Some of the Christians in ancient Corinth were guilty of turning the Lord's Supper into a time of gluttonous eating and drinking. As a result, God disciplined them by making some weak and others sick—even taking the lives of the more stubborn ones (1 Cor. 11:27–34). Their negative example and subsequent punishment should encourage us to celebrate communion with reverence and sincerity.

B. **Water baptism.** Throughout church history, Christians have made their commitment to Christ public by participating in water baptism. Whether by immersion, pouring, or sprinkling, the act of water baptism symbolizes the identification of the Christian with the death and resurrection of Jesus Christ.[1] Paul used this imagery when he wrote, "Do you not know that all of us who have been baptized into Christ Jesus have been baptized into His death? Therefore we have been buried with Him through baptism into death, in order that as Christ was raised from the dead through the glory of the Father, so we too might walk in newness of life" (Rom. 6:3–4). As with the Lord's Supper, water baptism is not a take-it-or-leave-it act. God expects us to be baptized as a public declaration of our faith in His Son.

IV. Long Live God's People!

Church buildings may crumble, congregations split, and ministers preach Christ with wrong motives, but through it all, God's people will continue to gather and serve their Lord worldwide until He returns. Think about your relationship to the Church and ask yourself these questions: Are you participating in the ongoing ministry of the Church by serving in a local church? Do you generously commit your talents and finances to your church? Do you pray for your church and restrain from offering destructive criticism about its ministry? Are you a good representative of your church to the community? Have you been baptized? Do you observe the Lord's Supper regularly, reflectively, and seriously? God wants His people to obey Him faithfully and joyously. If we keep in mind that He has made us a part of His glorious Body-building program, we will have little trouble desiring to serve Him gladly in a local church. So let's stand up and be counted with those Christians who have gone before us. Let's rise up and give three cheers for the Church.

Living Insights

Study One

Churches . . . they seem to be sprinkled throughout every country, city, and village. They come in different packages, with different brand names and different styles. Perhaps they are a lot like people—no two

Continued on next page

---

1. For a more complete discussion on the relationship between water baptism and salvation, see the study guide titled *Growing Up in God's Family*, ed. Bill Watkins, from the Bible-teaching ministry of Charles R. Swindoll (Fullerton, Calif.: Insight for Living, 1986), pp. 15–16.

are identical. And just as people trace their roots to better understand themselves, so may the Church benefit from discovering her heritage. Let's look back in history to review our exciting beginnings.

● Open your Bible to the beginning of the book of Acts. As you start to read, allow the following questions to aid you in pinpointing some important discoveries. Why is the Church significant? What is its purpose? What are water baptism and the Lord's Supper all about? Place your answers under the appropriate headings. Read as much of Acts as your time will allow. Our history is well worth exploring!

Three Cheers for the Church—The Acts of the Apostles

The Church's Purpose? _____

_____

_____

_____

_____

_____

Water Baptism? _____

_____

_____

_____

_____

The Lord's Supper? _____

_____

_____

_____

_____

Living Insights

In our previous study we looked at how baptism and the Lord's Supper were celebrated in the early Church. Let's move our time machine ahead nineteen hundred years and talk about how these church ordinances are celebrated today—especially in your life. Gather together some family or friends and discuss the following questions, keeping in mind two ground rules: (1) Don't put anyone down; help everyone feel comfortable and accepted. (2) Encourage all members of the group to participate; don't let any individuals "hog" the time.

- Have you been baptized? What were the circumstances surrounding your decision?
- What did your participation in baptism mean to you personally?
- How would you explain the significance of baptism to a six-year-old child?
- What was it like the first time you participated in the Lord's Supper?
- Have you ever taken the Lord's Supper in an unusual setting? Did the setting detract from or enhance the meaning?
- What significance does the Lord's Supper have for you personally?

Encouragement Served Family Style

Hebrews 10; Proverbs 10, 12, 18

When was the last time you were pierced by an unkind remark or unjustified criticism? Did it wound deeply? Do you still suffer from its effects? It seems we live in a world where the goal of life is to put down as many people as possible. Consequently, frustration and depression are running amok in our towns, offices, . . . even our homes. We need to find a place of refuge—a place, as one songwriter put it, "where seldom is heard a discouraging word." Not necessarily a place where, instead of people, "buffalo roam and the deer and the antelope play." God has a different setting in mind. According to His plan, the local church should shelter the discouraged and downcast. We shouldn't have to go to some idealized, peopleless range. If we could change the words of "Home on the Range" to express His thoughts, it might go like this:

> O give me a church where folks in the lurch
> Are encouraged, then healed from above;
> Where seldom is heard a discouraging word,
> And the truth is modeled in love.[1]

Is there such a place? Yes—in fact, there are many churches uplifting people. But even more congregations need to be filled with Christians committed to encouraging those around them. Let's dedicate ourselves to this needed ministry as we consider what Scripture says about it.

I. Encouragement Defined and Explained

Webster's dictionary says *encourage* means ". . . 1. To inspire with courage, spirit, or hope: hearten. 2. To spur on: stimulate. 3. To give help. . . ."[2] The term *enthusiasm* has a similar meaning. The Greek root of this word is *entheos,* which means "to put God (*theos*) into (*en*) something or someone." We can conclude from this that the basic meaning of *encouragement* is "to put courage into someone." The Greek words used in the New Testament for this term definitely bear out that understanding. Greek scholar William Barclay summarizes the usages of one such word:

> Again and again we find that *parakalein* ["encouragement"] is *the word of the rallying-call;* it is the word used of the speeches of leaders and of soldiers who urge each other on. It is the word used of words which send fearful

1. Charles R. Swindoll, *Growing Deep in the Christian Life* (Portland, Oreg.: Multnomah Press, 1986), p. 371.

2. Webster's Ninth New Collegiate Dictionary, s.v. "encourage."

and timorous and hesitant soldiers and sailors coura-
geously into battle. A *parakletos* is therefore an *encourager,* one who puts courage into the faint-hearted, one
who nerves the feeble arm for fight, one who makes a
very ordinary man cope gallantly with a perilous and a
dangerous situation. . . .

The word *parakalein* is the word for exhorting [others]
to noble deeds and high thoughts; it is especially the
word of courage before battle. Life is always calling us
into battle and the one who makes us able to stand up
to the opposing forces, to cope with life and to conquer
life is the *parakletos,* the Holy Spirit, who is none other
than the presence and the power of the risen Christ.[3]

II. The Biblical Basis for Encouragement

Many passages in Scripture spotlight the importance of encouragement in the family of God. One passage is Hebrews 10:24–25. These
verses follow a lengthy doctrinal section that establishes Jesus Christ
as superior to previous revelation (1:1–3), the angels (1:4–2:18),
Moses (3:1–19), Joshua (4:1–13), the Aaronic priesthood (4:14–7:28),
and the old covenant (8:1–10:18). The writer demonstrates that
Christ, through His death, has inaugurated a new covenant that provides for the forgiveness of all sins by faith in Him. In response to
these great truths, the writer exhorts us to obey three commands.

A. Draw near. "Let us draw near [to God] with a sincere heart
in full assurance of faith, having our hearts sprinkled clean from
an evil conscience and our bodies washed with pure water"
(10:22). These words urge us to claim the redemptive benefits
that are ours in Christ. We no longer have to suffer the pangs of
inward guilt and outward impurity. We can come before God in
prayer, realizing that He accepts us on the basis of His Son's sacrifice on the cross (1 John 1:7–9).

B. Hold fast. "Let us hold fast the confession of our hope without
wavering, for He who promised is faithful" (Heb. 10:23). We can
believe God will fulfill His promises because He has the knowledge, power, and desire to do so. Therefore, we should rely on
Him completely and tenaciously.

C. Encourage. "Let us consider how to stimulate one another to
love and good deeds, not forsaking our own assembling together,
as is the habit of some, but encouraging one another; and all the
more, as you see the day drawing near" (vv. 24–25). This last
command is on the same level as the other two. The writer calls
us to "consider how to *stimulate* one another" (emphasis added).

3. William Barclay, *More New Testament Words* (New York, N.Y.: Harper and Brother, 1958),
pp. 134–35.

The Greek word translated *stimulate* is usually used in a negative sense to mean "irritate" or "exasperate." But here it carries the idea of provoking, prodding, or inciting a fellow believer to exercise loving concern for other believers. The writer singles out one way to accomplish this—consistently meeting with other Christians in order to infuse them with courage to live godly lives. Woven in the fabric of this command are two thoughts we need to bring out.

1. **Encouragement is not the responsibility of a gifted few, but the responsibility of all in the family of God.** Not everyone is called to be a pastor, an elder, or a vocational Christian worker. But every believer is called to be an encourager.

2. **Encouragement is not something needed less in God's family, but something needed more.** We saw in a previous lesson that we are in "the last days" (2 Tim. 3:1, Heb. 1:2, 2 Pet. 3:3) and that this period will come to an end when Christ returns to defeat His enemies and establish His millennial reign (Rev. 19:11–20:4).[4] The closer this day of judgment comes, the more crucial it is that we encourage one another. For as this day draws nearer, the times will become increasingly more perilous, even savage (2 Tim. 3:1–8, Matt. 24:4–22). In such desperate times, we especially need our churches to be sanctuaries of encouragement—places where we're cared for, exhorted, and shown how to grow in biblical knowledge, love, and purity. We don't need sarcastic jabs, derogatory comments, and harsh judgments. We get enough of those from the world.

III. Encouragement: How to Do It

Now that we know God commands us to encourage others, let's consider how we can fulfill this important obligation. In fact, let's narrow our attention to an important vehicle of encouragement— the tongue. The Lord says a great deal about our words and the effect they have on the lives of others. Let's look at what He says in some passages from Proverbs.

A. **Proverbs 10:11–13a.** Here we're told that from "the mouth of the righteous" flows life-giving words of love, forgiveness, and wisdom. On the other hand, strife comes from the wicked, who are full of hatred and violence. One key, then, to having an encouraging tongue is ridding ourselves of bitterness and resentment—a

---

4. A clear, practical treatment of end-time events is given in the study guide *Daniel: God's Pattern for the Future,* ed. Bill Watkins, from the Bible-teaching ministry of Charles R. Swindoll (Fullerton, Calif.: Insight for Living, 1986).

process that involves confession before the Lord and forgiveness of others.

B. Proverbs 10:19–21a. This passage reminds us that a few well-chosen words are often more effective for godliness than paragraphs of counsel quickly given. Indeed, those who wisely ration their words bring treasured nourishment to hungry minds and hearts. Realizing this, we need to weigh our thoughts and express only those that edify, not those that destroy.

C. Proverbs 12:17–18. In these verses, we're told that speaking the truth is telling what is right. The writer quickly adds, however, that the truth should not be thrust like a sword into someone's side; rather, it should bring healing, like balm does to a painful wound. We can develop this kind of ministry as we grow in sensitivity to others and their needs.

D. Proverbs 18:21. This verse says that "death and life are in the power of the tongue, / And those who love it will eat its fruit." Death words tear down and create humiliating, hateful feelings. Life words, however, infuse courage and build strength of character. Whoever leans on our comments—our children, mates, work associates, or fellow Christians—will find in them either death or life, discouragement or encouragement, humiliation or edification. Of course, we cannot give courage transfusions if we lack confidence and self-esteem. We can only release what we have. Therefore, we need to see ourselves as God does—as objects of His love who are so precious that He sacrificed His Son for us. Now that's a solid foundation for self-worth![5]

IV. A Classic Example of an Encourager

The story of David and Jonathan perfectly illustrates encouragement at work. David, while he was still a teenager, killed the mightiest soldier in the Philistine army—Goliath (1 Sam. 17:1–51). This act of heroism brought him to the attention of both Saul, king of Israel, and Saul's son, Jonathan (17:55–18:5). Jonathan grew to love David as a loyal friend, while Saul became increasingly resentful toward David because of his popularity. It didn't take long before the king's hatred intensified to such a degree that David had to flee for his life. He found refuge from Saul's spear "in the wilderness of Ziph" (23:14). Confused and afraid, he was visited by Jonathan who "encouraged him in God" (v. 16). Jonathan strengthened David with words that

---

5. If you're struggling with self-worth or know someone who is, we recommend you consult the following sources: *One of a Kind: A Biblical View of Self-Acceptance,* by M. Blaine Smith (Downers Grove, Ill.: InterVarsity Press, 1984); *The Discovered Self: The Search for Self-Acceptance,* by Earl D. Wilson (Downers Grove, Ill.: InterVarsity Press, 1985); *In Search of Dignity,* by R. C. Sproul (Ventura, Calif.: Regal Books, 1983); *His Image, My Image,* by Josh McDowell (San Bernardino, Calif.: Here's Life Publishers, 1984).

were inspired by love and directed toward fear.[6] By doing so, he cut through the layers masking David's fear and ministered to his soul, giving him the courage to press on even in the face of a life-endangering situation. As wonderful as this was, Jonathan was not always able to be around to help his friend. On another occasion, David found himself standing alone against a large group of his own people who wanted to kill him. So without Jonathan, David "strengthened himself in the Lord his God" (30:6).

A Courage Transfusion for the Lonely

Like David, we, too, can find needed encouragement from God when we're struggling without human support. One way is through prayer. By "[drawing] near with confidence to the throne of grace, ... we may receive mercy and may find grace to help in time of need" (Heb. 4:16). Another way is to meditate on the Psalms. Every human emotion is expressed and every basic human need is met in this ancient hymnbook. Many people have found nourishment for their souls in its pages. Believers have also been uplifted by songs Christians have written about their faith. God often uses the message, melody, and rhythm of their music to soothe our fears, comfort our sorrows, and encourage our hearts. We are never completely alone or totally without support. The Lord is always with us, renewing our souls in many ways (Heb. 13:5–6).

V. Three Crucial Questions regarding Encouragement

Let's wrap up our thoughts in this lesson by addressing three practical questions.

A. Who should we attempt to encourage? Ideally, everyone we meet. But since this is not always possible, we need to strive for a more realistic goal—infusing courage into those with whom we have close relationships. Our friends, spouses, children, parents, brothers, and sisters ... these are all potential candidates for our encouragement ministry. Are you sensitive to the needs and fears of those around you? Are you reaching out especially to those you love most, or are they the last to receive encouraging words from you?

B. How can a person's protective emotional layers be penetrated? We all tend to hide our fears, even when we need them exposed for our welfare. But with sufficient time, patience, and compassion, our encouraging comments toward others can

---

6. Lawrence J. Crabb, Jr., and Dan B. Allender, *Encouragement: The Key to Caring* (Grand Rapids, Mich.: Zondervan Publishing House, 1984), p. 71.

eventually seep through the layers that cover their fear to nurture anew the strength they need to carry on.

C. What essential techniques need to be remembered?
Keeping in mind that encouragement is inspired by love and directed toward fear, here are six things we can do to ensure that our counsel is implanting courage.

1. **Talk less so we can feel and listen more.**
2. **Choose with sensitivity our times for speaking.**
3. **Avoid judging or condemning.**
4. **Examine our motives for helping.**
5. **Guard ourselves against sarcasm.**
6. **Refuse to hide behind our own layers of fear.**

This is how we can serve encouragement family style. Will you begin a ministry of encouragement today?

Living Insights

Study One ▪▪▪▪▪▪▪▪▪▪▪▪▪▪▪▪▪▪▪▪▪▪▪▪▪▪▪▪▪▪▪▪▪▪▪▪▪▪

Since the family of God should be filled with encouragers, we need to strive to meet our responsibilities in this area. Let's begin by probing into Proverbs so we can learn more about how to give courage transfusions.

- Rather than attempting to read through all the proverbs, let's zero in on chapters 15–18. Look for principles of encouragement and write them in the chart provided below. As a hint, look for words like *tongue, lips, answer, mouth,* and *words.*

Encouragement in Proverbs 15–18	
References	Principles

Continued on next page

References	Principles

🖐 *Living Insights*

Study Two ▬▬▬▬▬▬▬▬▬▬▬▬▬▬▬▬▬▬▬▬▬▬▬▬▬

Encouragement works best when it is both given and received. When you think back to uplifting moments in your life, you'll probably agree that they occurred not only when you were the one being encouraged but also when you were the encourager. As you try a few of the following suggestions for encouraging others, you just might discover that you are encouraged in the process.

- Encourage someone who has strengthened you. Express your appreciation for what that person has done for you in the past.
- Next Sunday, attempt to encourage two people in your congregation— the person you've known the longest and someone you've never met before.
- Try three different forms of encouragement. Encourage someone through spoken words . . . someone else through writing . . . another person through an act of kindness.
- Encourage your spiritual leaders by demonstrating your appreciation to your pastor, your Sunday School teacher, your Bible study leader, your radio Bible teacher, or your discipler.
- Sometimes it is most difficult to encourage the ones to whom we are closest. Go out of your way to show your appreciation and support of your family, roommates, or close friends.

Worship: Let It Shine!
Let It Shine!
Psalm 95:1–5

"The worship of God is the most blessed of all earthly vocations. There is no higher or nobler task to which we can give our energies and devote our time. God is first. God is worthy. And we are privileged to enjoy personal fellowship with Him."[1] If this is true, then why have some described worship as "the missing jewel of the evangelical Church"?[2] Why have so many churches today reduced worship to a Sunday morning ritual of rote singing and passive listening? Basically, they have forgotten that worship is a verb—it calls for action, vibrancy, and participation. We need to return to God's Word to examine and apply what it says about worship. Let's unearth again the sparkling jewel of worship—the gem that lights up our souls as we ascribe supreme worth to God. Our purpose will not be to discover a "worship package" offering mechanical, easy-to-follow steps on how to exalt God. Instead, let's direct our energy toward grasping the real meaning of worship—what its purpose is, why we should be involved in it, and how we can do it with sparkle.

I. The Jewel Rediscovered
Psalms is Scripture's worship hymnal, capturing not only the emotion of worship but also its essence, significance, and purpose. Let's turn to its pages to rediscover the missing jewel of today's church.

A. Worship's identity and meaning. Psalm 95 opens with an invitation to worship the Lord:
> "O come, let us sing for joy to the Lord;
> Let us shout joyfully to the rock of our salvation.
> Let us come before His presence with thanksgiving;
> Let us shout joyfully to Him with psalms." (vv. 1–2)

Why should we accept the psalmist's invitation? Because
> "the Lord is a great God,
> And a great King above all gods,
> In whose hand are the depths of the earth;
> The peaks of the mountains are His also.
> The sea is His, for it was He who made it;
> And His hands formed the dry land." (vv. 3–5)

Anyone as great and powerful as God deserves our meditative, melodious, even shouting praise. We should kneel and bow before Him in abject submission and joyful adoration (vv. 1–2, 6). As

---

1. Ronald Allen and Gordon Borror, *Worship: Rediscovering the Missing Jewel,* A Critical Concern Book (Portland, Oreg.: Multnomah Press, 1982), p. 10.

2. A. W. Tozer, *Worship: The Missing Jewel of the Evangelical Church* (Harrisburg, Penn.: Christian Publications, n.d.), as quoted by Allen and Borror in *Worship,* p. 7.

we do, we will "connect" with Him in such a way that we will feel as if we could reach out and touch Him; we will become pre-occupied with the Lord. That's what worship is about. Put briefly, *worship is a human response to a divine revelation.* Sometimes we should worship in quiet meditation; at other times, with joyful shouting or robust singing. However it's expressed, worship is our way of actively acknowledging the supreme *worth-ship* of God, opening the door for Him to touch us, to fill us with His peaceful, reassuring presence.

B. Worship's significance and purpose. The purpose of worship is bound up with the product of worship. It doesn't make any difference whether we worship alone, in a small group, or in a large gathering; our adoration causes several things to occur.

1. **Worship magnifies our God.** When we are in His presence, everything else takes its proper place under Him.

2. **Worship enlarges our horizons.** We begin to see beyond our limitations, catching a vision of His boundless perspective and resources.

3. **Worship eclipses our fears.** It helps us see that He has the means to meet all our needs and calm all our anxieties.

4. **Worship changes our perspective.** We start to view the here and now from the standpoint of the there and then. The temporal takes on limited significance, while the eternal begins to alter our lives.

5. **Worship refreshes our spirit.** We come into God's presence burdened by sin and our worries; we leave His presence clean and at peace, ready to face the challenges of another day.

6. **Worship enhances our work.** It gives our labors eternal value, for it shows us that they are a means of glorifying Him (1 Cor. 10:31, Col. 3:17).

7. **Worship highlights our music.** Singing and playing instruments should not be considered time-fillers or preliminaries to the sermon. Music is an essential part of exalting God (Pss. 92:1–4, 150:3–6). We should often raise our voices and instruments in resonant praise of the Lord. Unfortunately, however, our musical worship is usually limited to Sunday. Why? Frequently it's because we allow life's daily pressures to squeeze out our song. Rather than casting our worries on God, we hold on to them, squelching the relaxation we need for creative worship. Another reason we so seldom sing is that someone else is always singing for us. Wherever we go—be it the grocery store, doctor's office, workplace, even the elevator—music is being forced into our lives. *We*

need to start singing to God again—regularly. Perhaps we should listen to the car radio and home stereo less so we can sing praises more. It might even be helpful to purchase a hymnbook or two and sing songs from it in our personal or family devotions. In whatever way we choose to replenish our lives with music of adoration to Him, we will find needed renewal and encouragement.

II. Some Often-Overlooked Facets of the Jewel

There are at least three facts about worship that can raise our appreciation of its value and motivate us to make it a vital part of our daily lives.

A. Worship is sought by God. The Lord Jesus Christ not only accepted worship of Himself (Matt. 14:33, John 9:38) but also engaged in worshiping His Father (Matt. 14:23; Mark 1:35, 14:36; John 17). When Christ spoke about worship, He mentioned two essential ingredients (John 4:24). One is adoring God in *truth*—basing our veneration on His written Word, the Bible. The other is worshiping Him in *spirit.* Since this has to do with the realm of the invisible, it probably includes our imagination. Our ability to fantasize can help us experience the feelings expressed in a song, a prayer, or a Bible passage. Mental images can connect us to God, adding new depth to our worship. And when our minds are filled with the truth of His Word, our imaginations will have the fuel they need to soar freely and creatively in their exaltation of Him.

B. Worship has been practiced in the past. Throughout history, people have raised their eyes toward heaven and praised God's holy name. Many have revered God in response to His mighty works (Exod. 15:1–21, 2 Chron. 5:1–7:10, Neh. 8–9); some have worshiped with the expectation of great personal sacrifice (Gen. 22:5–13, Dan. 6:6–16); others, during times of tremendous suffering (Job 1:6–22). Regardless of the circumstances or the cost, believers throughout time have honored the Lord with their worship.[3] For you see, worship doesn't require comfortable surroundings, organ music, and a choir. All that's needed is one person with a desire to praise God in spirit and in truth.

C. Worship is needed in the present. Romans 12:1 says, "I urge you therefore, brethren, by the mercies of God, to present your bodies a living and holy sacrifice, acceptable to God, which

---

3. Some excellent books on the history of worship are: *Worship in the Early Church,* by Ralph P. Martin (1964; reprint, Grand Rapids, Mich.: William B. Eerdmans Publishing Co., 1978); *In His Presence: Appreciating Your Worship Tradition,* by Robert N. Schaper (Nashville, Tenn.: Thomas Nelson Publishers, 1984); and *Worship Old and New,* by Robert E. Webber (Grand Rapids, Mich.: Ministry Resources Library, Zondervan Publishing House, 1982).

is your spiritual service of worship." This verse exhorts all Christians to worship God through who they are and what they do. Everyday life can be transformed into an act of worship. In our homes, offices, churches, schools, even recreation centers, we can glorify the Lord by being and behaving godly. This idea will revolutionize our lives if we will only take it to heart and make it part of our walk with Him.

III. The Sparkling Beauty of the Rediscovered Jewel

Perhaps worship has been a missing jewel in your life. The wonderful news is that it does not have to remain lost; you can rediscover it for yourself. Use these three closing questions to help you relocate the gem that can illuminate your life.

A. Does your public worship sparkle with creativity and variety? One way to help this happen is to allow the music of the worship service to speak to you and move you. Become personally involved in the lyrics, the melody, and the rhythm, responding through them with praise to God.

B. Does your private worship sparkle with quality and consistency? It can, if you will give it the importance it deserves in your life.

C. Has something taken the sparkle out of your worship? If so, find out what it is and remove it from your life. Do everything you can to let the jewel of worship shine once again in your experience of God. Through active worship, you display your love for the Lord and your commitment to obeying His Word. Let it shine!

Living Insights

Study One

Do you know what you've just done? You've just worked through the ten major doctrines of the Christian faith! Congratulations are in order for all of you who have diligently finished this important study. Before we conclude, though, we need to take a final exam—like our midterm a few lessons back. But relax. You can use your notes!

- Let's take a few minutes to review what we've learned. With the help of your Bible and study guide, find one important *truth* from each of the ten messages listed here and write it in the space provided. It may be an aspect of doctrine you learned for the first time, or perhaps it's a truth you rediscovered.

GROWING DEEP IN THE CHRISTIAN LIFE
Salvation

"Mr. Smith, Meet Your Substitute" _____

_____

_____

_____

The Remedy for Our Disease _____

_____

_____

_____

The Return of Christ

His Coming Is Sure . . . Are You? _____

_____

_____

_____

Until He Returns . . . What? _____

_____

_____

_____

Resurrection

Visiting the *Real* Twilight Zone _____

_____

_____

_____

An Interview with One from Beyond _____

_____

_____

Continued on next page

163

The Body of Christ

God's Body-building Program _____

_____

_____

_____

Three Cheers for the Church _____

_____

_____

_____

The Family of God

Encouragement Served Family Style _____

_____

_____

_____

Worship: Let It Shine! Let It Shine! _____

_____

_____

_____

 Living Insights

Study Two ▬▬▬▬▬▬▬▬▬▬▬▬▬▬▬▬▬▬▬▬▬▬

Let's continue with the second part of our final exam. In study one, we looked at the significant truths we had learned in the last half of this series. Now we want to turn our attention to the realm of application.

- How did your life change as a result of these messages? Is there a meaningful *application* you can point to in each one? Use the same procedure you used in study one and list your findings in the blanks provided.

"Mr. Smith, Meet Your Substitute" _____

_____

_____

_____

The Remedy for Our Disease _____

_____

_____

_____

The Return of Christ

His Coming Is Sure . . . Are You? _____

_____

_____

_____

Until He Returns . . . What? _____

_____

_____

_____

Resurrection

Visiting the *Real* Twilight Zone _____

_____

_____

_____

An Interview with One from Beyond _____

_____

_____

Continued on next page

The Body of Christ

God's Body-building Program _____

_____

_____

_____

Three Cheers for the Church _____

_____

_____

_____

The Family of God

Encouragement Served Family Style _____

_____

_____

_____

Worship: Let It Shine! Let It Shine! _____

_____

_____

_____

Books for Probing Further

Whew! We've covered a lot of ground in this doctrinal series. But you know, we've only scratched the surface. Hopefully, our study has renewed your appreciation of theology and its practical implications. Without healthy roots, we can hardly expect to grow healthy fruit. However, there is much more to discover and apply in the rich soil of Christian truth. The following list of books has been put together with this goal in mind. Your roots can never penetrate too deeply into theology as long as the fruit of that knowledge is application. And as you increasingly learn and put to use more of God's truth, you will become "like a tree firmly planted by streams of water, / Which yields its fruit in its season, / And its leaf does not wither; / And in whatever [you do, you will prosper]" (Ps. 1:3).

I. Growing Deeper in Theology

Chafer, Lewis Sperry. *Major Bible Themes.* Revised by John F. Walvoord. Grand Rapids, Mich.: Zondervan Publishing House, 1974. This book concisely and accurately covers fifty-two key Christian doctrines. It's an indispensable guide for the person who wants to know what the Bible teaches.

Little, Paul E. *Know What You Believe.* Wheaton, Ill.: Victor Books, 1985. Few books cover as much theological territory in down-to-earth terms as this one does. Whether you're new to Christian doctrine or just a bit rusty, this book will help you gain a theological foothold in basic biblical truth.

Thiessen, Henry C. *Lectures in Systematic Theology.* Revised by Vernon D. Doerksen. Grand Rapids, Mich.: William B. Eerdmans Publishing Co., 1979. This book provides a balanced, clear, practical treatment of the major doctrines of the Christian faith.

II. Growing Deeper in the Doctrine of the Bible

Geisler, Norman L., and William E. Nix. *A General Introduction to the Bible.* Revised edition. Chicago, Ill.: Moody Press, 1986. Undoubtedly, this is one of the most comprehensive, up-to-date, and useful books in print on the inspiration, canonization, transmission, and translation of the Bible.

Geisler, Norman L., ed. *Inerrancy.* Grand Rapids, Mich.: Zondervan Publishing House, 1979. Various evangelical scholars join forces in this book to present a readable and reasonable defense of the inerrancy of Scripture.

Pache, René. *The Inspiration and Authority of Scripture.* Translated by Helen I. Needham. Chicago, Ill.: Moody Press, 1969. The author combines sound scholarship and an easy-to-read style to present an excellent explanation and defense of the Bible as God's authoritative Word to man.

III. Growing Deeper in the Doctrine of God

Bavinck, Herman. *The Doctrine of God.* Translated by William Hendriksen. Grand Rapids, Mich.: Baker Book House, 1979. This classic book is not light reading, but you will come away from it with a sound and reverent biblical understanding of the Lord of Lords.

Packer, J. I. *Knowing God.* Downers Grove, Ill.: InterVarsity Press, 1973. Packer will not only inform your mind but fire your heart. His book is a must for anyone who really wants to know God.

Sproul, R. C. *The Holiness of God.* Wheaton, Ill.: Tyndale House Publishers, 1985. Chuck Colson has said of this book, "[It] drove me to my knees and dramatically changed my Christian life. Written by one of the most brilliant thinkers of our day, it is absolutely urgent reading for every Christian."

IV. Growing Deeper in the Doctrine of Christ

Craig, William Lane. *The Son Rises: Historical Evidence for the Resurrection of Jesus.* Chicago, Ill.: Moody Press, 1981. The resurrection of Christ is certainly the greatest demonstration of His deity available to us. Craig does a masterful job setting forth the mountain of evidence for the historicity of this unique miracle. He also clearly explains the significance of this event for us today.

Culver, Robert Duncan. *The Life of Christ.* Grand Rapids, Mich.: Baker Book House, 1976. To accurately grasp who Christ is and what difference He makes, we need to know about His life on earth. Culver retells the story of Jesus' life, drawing on recent historical and archaeological discoveries that enrich our understanding of Christ and the culture in which He ministered.

Walvoord, John F. *Jesus Christ Our Lord.* Chicago, Ill.: Moody Press, 1969. This book provides a systematic, biblical, insightful treatment of the doctrine of Christ. It covers not only Jesus' life on earth but also His existence before the world's creation and His future life as ruler of the new heavens and new earth.

V. Growing Deeper in the Doctrine of the Holy Spirit

Packer, J. I. *Keep In Step with the Spirit.* Old Tappan, N.J.: Fleming H. Revell Co., 1984. This is a thought-provoking and illuminating book on the Holy Spirit. Not everyone will agree with all of Packer's conclusions, but few will walk away from his book unmotivated to allow the Spirit more control over their lives.

Walvoord, John F. *The Holy Spirit.* 3d ed. Grand Rapids, Mich.: Zondervan Publishing House, 1958. Walvoord provides an extensive treatment of the doctrine of the Holy Spirit, employing an uncommon grasp of Scripture's collective teachings on this subject.

Wood, Leon J. *The Holy Spirit in the Old Testament.* Grand Rapids, Mich.: Zondervan Publishing House, 1976. The Old Testament's teaching about the Holy Spirit is generally neglected today, while the New Testament's instruction is presented often but commonly misunderstood. Wood's book helps solve both these problems by giving a careful and insightful presentation of the doctrine of God's Spirit as set forth in the Old Testament and illuminated in the New.

VI. Growing Deeper in the Doctrine of Man

Allen, Ronald B. *The Majesty of Man: The Dignity of Being Human.* A Critical Concern Book. Portland, Oreg.: Multnomah Press, 1984. In an age of confusion about the nature, purpose, and dignity of man, Allen clears away the fog with a scripturally balanced portrait.

Blocher, Henri. *In the Beginning: The Opening Chapters of Genesis.* Translated by David G. Preston. Downers Grove, Ill.: InterVarsity Press, 1984. Blocher supplies a detailed study of the first several chapters of Genesis, giving us a valuable understanding of man's origin, nature, significance, fall, and restoration.

Custance, Arthur C. *Genesis and Early Man.* Vol. 2 of *The Doorway Papers.* Grand Rapids, Mich.: Academie Books, Zondervan Publishing House, 1975. Anthropologist and theologian Arthur Custance tackles the evolutionary theories about man head-on and demonstrates the scientific validity of the biblical view of man.

VII. Growing Deeper in the Doctrine of Salvation

Chafer, Lewis Sperry. *Salvation: A Clear Doctrinal Analysis.* Grand Rapids, Mich.: Academie Books, Zondervan Publishing House, 1945. This is a fine handbook on salvation and the eternal security of the believer.

Lightner, Robert P. *The Death Christ Died: A Case for Unlimited Atonement.* Schaumburg, Ill.: Regular Baptist Press, 1967. The author demonstrates with sound reason and accurate exegesis that Christ died for all mankind, not just for those God knew would be saved.

Pentecost, J. Dwight. *Things Which Become Sound Doctrine.* Grand Rapids, Mich.: Zondervan Publishing House, 1965. The plan of salvation covers not only conversion but sanctification and glorification as well. In this book, Pentecost presents simply and practically God's whole redemption plan.

VIII. Growing Deeper in the Doctrine of Christ's Return

Archer, Gleason L., Jr. et al. *The Rapture: Pre-, Mid-, or Post-Tribulational?* Grand Rapids, Mich.: Academie Books, Zondervan Publishing House, 1984. With a rigorous, yet respectful, spirit of give-and-take, three evangelical scholars present and defend their positions on the Rapture's relationship to the Great Tribulation.

Clouse, Robert G., ed. *The Meaning of the Millennium: Four Views.* Downers Grove, Ill.: InterVarsity Press, 1977. Here the views of historic premillennialism, dispensational premillennialism, post-millennialism, and amillennialism are clearly explained and defended by some of their best advocates.

Hoyt, Herman A. *The End Times.* Chicago, Ill.: Moody Press, 1969. The author unfolds a panoramic perspective of the future, which includes a pretribulational view of Christ's return.

IX. Growing Deeper in the Doctrine of Man's Resurrection

Anderson, J. Kerby. *Life, Death and Beyond.* Grand Rapids, Mich.: Zondervan Publishing House, 1980. In this book, dying, death, and the afterlife are discussed from cultural, medical, and biblical standpoints. The result is a comprehensive, up-to-date, and practical treatment of our destiny.

Harris, Murray J. *Raised Immortal: Resurrection and Immortality in the New Testament.* Grand Rapids, Mich.: William B. Eerdmans Publishing Co., 1983. The answers to every question you've ever asked about the New Testament's teaching on resurrection and immortality can be found in this book. Not a book to be read quickly, it provides profound insight and understanding of two topics that are often neglected and misunderstood.

Kreeft, Peter J. *Heaven, the Heart's Deepest Longing.* San Francisco, Calif.: Harper and Row, 1980. Until the publication of this book, nothing of much substance was in print on the Christian doctrine of heaven. Kreeft has done us a great service by writing an illuminating and exciting book on the "country" we long to see and enjoy.

X. Growing Deeper in the Doctrine of the Church

Heritage of Freedom. Belleville, Mich.: Lion Publishing Corp., 1984. This book provides a beautifully illustrated survey of some of the people who have helped shape the Church and the world from the second century to the present. In reading it, we can better appreciate the differences in the contemporary Church by gaining an understanding of its past.

Saucy, Robert L. *The Church in God's Program.* Chicago, Ill.: Moody Press, 1972. The author lays bare the Bible's teaching on the nature, origin, organization, ministry, and worship of the universal Church and the local church.

Stott, John. *One People.* Revised edition. Old Tappan, N.J.: Fleming H. Revell Co., 1982. Stott explains that every Christian is a minister. And the goal of every church is to enable and equip all of its members to become the ministers God wants them to be. Stott presents the biblical case for this position and gives the guidelines necessary to move it from theory to everyday practice.

Insight for Living
Cassette Tapes
Growing Deep in the Christian Life
Returning to Our Roots

The backbone of our faith is biblical doctrine—objective truth, not subjective feelings. These all-important theological issues give us stability against the strong currents of our day. This series will help equip you with scriptural facts and practical insights. As you learn these doctrines, you will become "like a tree firmly planted," with roots nourished in God's inerrant Word.

			U.S.	Canadian
GCL	CS	Cassette series—includes album cover	$60.25	$76.50
		Individual cassettes—include messages A and B	5.00	6.35

These prices are effective as of March 1987 and are subject to change without notice.

GCL   **1-A:** *The Value of Knowing the Scoop*—Selected Scripture
      B: *Don't Forget to Add a Cup of Discernment*—Selected Scripture

GCL   **2-A:** *God's Book—God's Voice*—Psalm 119
      B: *Handling the Scriptures Accurately*—Matthew 9, 12, 15, 16; Nehemiah 8

GCL   **3-A:** *Knowing God: Life's Major Pursuit*—Jeremiah 9:23–24, 29:11–14
      B: *Loving God: Our Ultimate Response*—Deuteronomy 6:4–9, Selected Psalms

GCL   **4-A:** *Mary's Little Lamb*—Luke 2, Micah 5, Isaiah 7
      B: *When the God-Man Walked among Us*—Selections from the Gospels

GCL   **5-A:** *Changing Lives Is Jesus' Business*—John 4, 9, 20
      B: *The Spirit Who Is Not a Ghost*—John 16:1–15

GCL   **6-A:** *From Creation to Corruption*—Genesis 1–5; Romans 3, 5, 6
      B: *Exposing the Dark Side*—Selected Scripture

GCL   **7-A:** *"Mr. Smith, Meet Your Substitute"*—Romans 3
      B: *The Remedy for Our Disease*—Isaiah 53, Leviticus, Hebrews

GCL   **8-A:** *His Coming Is Sure . . . Are You?*—Selected Scripture
      B: *Until He Returns . . . What?*—Selected Scripture

GCL   **9-A:** *Visiting the Real Twilight Zone*—Selected Scripture
      B: *An Interview with One from Beyond*—Luke 16

GCL   **10-A:** *God's Body-building Program*—Matthew 16:16–18, Acts, 1 Corinthians
      B: *Three Cheers for the Church*—Philippians 1

GCL   **11-A:** *Encouragement Served Family Style*—Hebrews 10; Proverbs 10, 12, 18
      B: *Worship: Let It Shine! Let It Shine!*—Psalm 95:1–5

Ordering Information

U.S. ordering information: You are welcome to use our toll-free number (for Visa and MasterCard orders only) between the hours of 8:30 A.M. and 4:00 P.M., Pacific time, Monday through Friday. The number is **(800) 772-8888.** This number may be used anywhere in the continental United States except California, Hawaii, and Alaska. Orders from these areas are handled through our Sales Department at **(714) 870-9161.** We are unable to accept collect calls.

Your order will be processed promptly. We ask that you allow four to six weeks for delivery by fourth-class mail. If you wish your order to be shipped first-class, please add 10 percent of the total order cost (not including California sales tax) for shipping and handling.

Canadian ordering information: Your order will be processed promptly. We ask that you allow approximately four weeks for delivery by first-class mail to the U.S./Canadian border. All orders will be shipped from our office in Fullerton, California. For our listeners in British Columbia, a 7 percent sales tax must be added to the total of all tape orders (not including first-class postage). For further information, please contact our office at **(604) 272-5811.**

Payment options: We accept personal checks, money orders, Visa, and MasterCard in payment for materials ordered. Unfortunately, we are unable to offer invoicing or COD orders. If the amount of your check or money order is less than the amount of your purchase, your check will be returned so that you may place your order again with the correct amount. All orders must be paid in full before shipment can be made.

Returned checks: There is a $10 charge for any returned check (regardless of the amount of your order) to cover processing and invoicing.

Guarantee: Our tapes are guaranteed for ninety days against faulty performance or breakage due to a defect in the tape. For best results, please be sure your tape recorder is in good operating condition and is cleaned regularly.

Mail your order to one of the following addresses:

Insight for Living
Sales Department
Post Office Box 4444
Fullerton, CA 92634

Insight for Living Ministries
Post Office Box 2510
Vancouver, BC
Canada V6B 3W7

Quantity discounts and gift certificates are available upon request.

Overseas ordering information is provided on the reverse side of the order form.

Order Form

Please send me the following cassette tapes:

The current series: ☐ GCL CS Growing Deep in the Christian Life

Individual cassettes: ☐ GCL 1 ☐ GCL 2 ☐ GCL 3 ☐ GCL 4
☐ GCL 5 ☐ GCL 6 ☐ GCL 7 ☐ GCL 8
☐ GCL 9 ☐ GCL 10 ☐ GCL 11

I am enclosing:

$_____ To purchase the cassette series for $60.25 (in Canada $76.50*) which includes the album cover

$_____ To purchase individual tapes at $5.00 each (in Canada $6.35*)

$_____ Total of purchases

$_____ If the order will be delivered in California, please add 6 percent sales tax

$_____ U.S. residents please add 10 percent for first-class shipping and handling if desired

$_____ *British Columbia residents please add 7 percent sales tax

$_____ Canadian residents please add 6 percent for postage

$_____ **Overseas residents please add appropriate postage** (See postage chart under "Overseas Ordering Information.")

$_____ As a gift to the Insight for Living radio ministry for which a tax-deductible receipt will be issued

$_____ **Total amount due (Please do not send cash.)**

Form of payment:

☐ Check or money order made payable to Insight for Living

☐ Credit card (Visa or MasterCard only)

If there is a balance: ☐ apply it as a donation ☐ please refund

---

Credit card purchases:

☐ Visa ☐ MasterCard number _____

Expiration date _____

Signature _____

We cannot process your credit card purchase without your signature.

Name _____

Address _____

_____

City _____

State/Province _____ Zip/Postal code _____

Country _____

Telephone ( ) _____ Radio station ___ ___ ___ ___

Should questions arise concerning your order, we may need to contact you.

Overseas Ordering Information

If you do not live in the United States or Canada, please note the following information. This will ensure efficient processing of your request.

Estimated time of delivery: We ask that you allow approximately twelve to sixteen weeks for delivery by surface mail. If you would like your order sent airmail, the length of delivery may be reduced. All orders will be shipped from our office in Fullerton, California.

Payment options: Due to fluctuating currency rates, we can accept only personal checks made payable in U.S. funds, international money orders, Visa, and MasterCard in payment for materials ordered. If the amount of your check or money order is less than the amount of your purchase, your check will be returned so that you may place your order again with the correct amount. All orders must be paid in full before shipment can be made.

Returned checks: There is a $10 charge for any returned check (regardless of the amount of your order) to cover processing and invoicing.

Postage and handling: Please add to the amount of purchase the postage cost for the service you desire. All orders must include postage based on the chart below.

Purchase Amount		Surface Postage	Airmail Postage
From	To	Percentage of Order	Percentage of Order
$ .01	$15.00	40%	75%
15.01	75.00	25%	45%
75.01	or more	15%	40%

Guarantee: Our tapes are guaranteed for ninety days against faulty performance or breakage due to a defect in the tape. For best results, please be sure your tape recorder is in good operating condition and is cleaned regularly.

Mail your order or inquiry to the following address:

Insight for Living
Sales Department
Post Office Box 4444
Fullerton, CA 92634

Quantity discounts and gift certificates are available upon request.